¡VIVA! Tradiciones

THE JUNIOR LEAGUE OF CORPUS CHRISTI, INC.

The Junior League of Corpus Christi, Inc. is an organization of women committed to promoting voluntarism, to developing the potential of women, and to improving the community through the effective action and leadership of trained volunteers. Its purpose is exclusively educational and charitable.

For information on purchasing additional copies please write or call:

The Junior League of Corpus Christi, Inc.
P.O. Box 837
Corpus Christi, Texas 78403
1-800-884-3315
www.jlcc.org

ISBN: 0-9609144-2-0

First Printing   15,000 copies   1996
Second Printing   10,000 copies   1998

541 Doubletree Drive
Highland Village TX 75067
(972) 317-0245

Table of Contents

¡VIVA! South Texas

Long live our traditions, our communities and our families. The Junior League of Corpus Christi is proud to bring you a book that will reveal the riches of our varied ethnic heritage, the bounty of the gulf waters and the treasures of our ranches and farms. This unique combination of our community is reflected in the food we eat and by the way we live. We raise our glass to salute the spirit of charity and voluntarism, families, health and happiness. More present today than ever before is the need to incorporate the traditions of our ancestors and live happily in this fast paced world. We hope you will find in this book the flavors of the South Texas lifestyles that can be shared with our friends and families.

¡VIVA!

The Junior League of Corpus Christi is grateful to our artist and inspiration, Katie Willis! Katie has lovingly captured a glimpse of South Texas, our traditions, heritage and visual flavor with her contribution to ¡VIVA! TRADICIONES. She has been an imaginative influence throughout the development of this cookbook.

Katie was born and raised in Midland, Texas. She is a graduate of Salem College, Winston-Salem, North Carolina with a B.F.A. in Studio Arts. Serving as principal artist and co-owner, Katie created Gooseberry Pie, a stationery company, that enjoyed national and international success. Katie now lives in Corpus Christi, Texas with her husband, Richard and two sons, Turner and Buckley. Her talents are visible throughout this community with her continued involvement in voluntarism and the advancement of fine arts.

During the development of VIVA, in August of 1995, Katie was diagnosed with breast cancer. She met her illness with heart, resolute grace, and courage. We join Katie in her advocacy to encourage all women to practice breast self-examination and to have mammograms for the early detection and prevention of breast cancer. We are thankful for her recovery and inspired by her commitment to living life to its fullest potential.

¡VIVA KATIE!

Contributors

Cathy Abernethy
Jeanne Adams
Ann Ahuero
Phyllis Coffee Allen
Janet Gowdey Allen
Caroline Davy Altheide
Clare Anderson
Peggy Roberts Ansel
Joanne Arnold
Sydna Klingaman Arnold
Gay Griffith Ashmore
Terry Baiamonte
Debbie Baldwin
Tracey Barre
Joan Baskin
Suzy Scibienski Bass
Gretchen Benkendorfer
Courtenay Capt Berry
Shawn Bevly-Groesbeck
Corinne Vauter Biel
Joan Black
Corol Jo Blake
Kathleen Roscoe Boeck
Barbie Boeck
Carolyn Newton Boller
Martha Bonilla
Gail Webster Boynton
Bongie Anderson Bracy
Mary Jo Branscomb
Margaret Null Braselton
Lora Lou Brin
Catherine Counts Brooks
Diana Adams Broyles
Renee T. Burris
Jane C. Butt
Sheryl Calhoun
Sue McNeil Carey
Jennifer W. Carmer
Betsy Carrell
Robin Carter
Peggy Clark
Agatha Clements
Bonnie Cohen
Leah Cohen
Janey Davy Cone
Paula Cook
Jean Flint Cotten
Susan G. Dahlman
Jayne Davenport
Kathy Jones Davies
Becky Davis
Carol Anne Theis Davis
Kathleen Day
Mary Beth Delano
Beth Dietze
Jane B. Dodson
Terri Dupriest
Jerry Dyer
Julie A. Eberhard
Katy Haden Einspanier
Pat P. Eldridge
Ira Lee Ellis
Ralph Ellis
Debbi Ellwood

Cathy Stovall Elzner
Sharon Emerson
Anna Englehardt
Karen Brooks Erixon
Claire Essing
Cilia Fancher
Debbie Dulske Farenthold
Jessica Farrell
Brigid Ferguson
Cheryl Aymond Fetsis
Alice Ann Fisher
Amy Floyd
Ann Speckels Fox
Cornelia Herz Freeman
Beth Gaddie
Cindy Fernandez Gamez
Nancy Bluntzer Gandy
Lavonne Stewart Garrison
Rose Cavada Garza
Carolyn George
Renee George
Michelle Germano
Carol Dawson Giddings
Debbie Gilmore
Peggy Glisson
Elizabeth Vickers Goad
Linda S. Golden
Susan Goolishian
Roberta (Bo) Granberry
Glenda Gregorcyk
Gary Groesbeck
Dee Hargis
Claudia Blucher Harrell
Pamela Harrison
Jeanne Hart
Ione Harvey
Kathryn Hayes
Carrie Carrillo Heckman
Susan McElhaney Heinz
Carol Heinzelmann
Jaye McLelland Hellums
C.M. (Skip) Henkel III
Charlotte Ogden Henry
Diane Hermansen
Nancy Herring
Kathy Heymann
Kim W. Hill
Sarah Hill
Bobbye Clifton Hilliard
Jennifer Hilliard
Oline Hitchens
Nancy Hoblit
Kathy Hogan
Shirley Dawson Holt
Trish Hopkins
Melinda Arnold Houser
Karen Humphrey
Josephine P. Hurd
Elisha Tompkins Inserni
Bertha Ireman
Josie Jackson
Lucille Jackson
Renee Jasso
Carolyn Blake Johnston
David Johnston
Mary Helen Johnston
Rachel Jones

Jena Pickett Kauffmann
Betty Ellis Kepp
Rose Mary Keys
Macy Kinzel
Doral Knolle
Karen H. Knox
Kathy Kramer
Dixie Southerland Langley
Martha Fry Lewis
Susan Lewis
Betty Grett Lipstreu
Julie Little
Catherine Lundberg
Dana Lundgren
Greer M. Mahaffey
Jessica Mahaffey
Lynn Mahaffey
Patty Manzano
Carroll Patton Matthews
Shannon Pettus Mayo
Martha Maza
Refugio Maza
Nancy McBroom
Sandra S. McBurnett
Sue Farenthold McCauley
Sally McClure
Kathy McCord
Kathryn Ann McCracken
Lucy McCracken
Vera McGonigle
Mary Ann Harris McGregor
Sheryl McMillan
Julie McNeil
Crystal Mead
Michelle Merkle
Molly Watten Merkle
Joyce Meyers
Anne Attwell Montgomery
Linda Montoya
Laura Moore
Marilyn Munroe
SeSee Munson
Harriet H. Nelson
Karen Arnold Nicholson
Pamela Kubala Nye
Kary Klingaman O'Hair
Lisa O'Hair
Marilyn O'Keefe
Jon Ogg
Mary Ann Ekstrom Peck
Barbara Pender
Kristen Phelps
Rebecca Arnold Phillips
Laura Piper
Sue Pitcairn
Kelli Powell
Janet Pratt
Sylvia Prezas
Ella Wall Prichard
Marjorie Prichard
Shannon Ramsey
Geri Rice
Lisa Roberson
Marsha Nolen Robertson
Shelia Rogers
Marjorie Roscoe
Paula Rosenstein

Debbie Ross
Rosine Shindler Runyon
Joanne Salge
Claire Samo
Leslie J. Schnake
Cathy Scholl
Sandra Schultz
Paige Sciantarelli
Claudia Cook Shoemaker
Elizabeth Hunter Shoemaker
Melodi Eberle Sigler
Oralia Silvas
Paula Fitzhugh Singleton
Jenny Skrobarczyk
Mary Pat Slavik
Dixie Smith
Laura Smith
Mary Mendleski Smith
Virginia Solis
Crhisten Sorrell
Kimberly Davis Stockseth
Steven Wayne Stockseth
Dody Stofer
Lisa Strickhausen
Susan Susser
Larken Sutherland
Helen Scibienski Swetman
Etheleen Taggart
Daryl Hause Tanner
Celia Sexton Tate
Amy Taylor
Jane Stewart Taylor
Marcie Taylor
Sue Rosson Tejml
Sheila Perry Thomas
Carol Thorpe
Perry Tompkins
Candy Hurd Trask
Leigh Bentley Trcka
Billy Faye Tucker
Paula Turcotte
Sharon Vasquez
Sally Wallace
Ada Wallin
Bechy Warren
Suzi Smith Warzecha
Margaret Watkins
Jane M. Weathered
Jane Webb
Karen Stetter Welder
Kay Andrews Wenger
Sandy Wheeler
Marsha Wheless
Patricia Heaney White
Sylvia A. Whitmore
Karen Williams
Melanie Williams
Karla Wilson
Cindy Wintermute
Lorry Winters
Mary Sue Ogg Wisdom
Sara Wolter
Frances Overton Wolter
Ruth Woolsey
Karen Shaw Wuthrich
Marilynn G. Yankee
Mary Alice Young
Carole Zanetti
Carol Ann Jarvis Zeitler

¡VIVA! Cookbook Committee

1993-1994

Carolyn Blake Johnston ...... Chairman
Kimberly Davis Stockseth ... Treasurer

1994-1995

Carolyn Blake Johnston ...... Chairman
Kimberly Davis Stockseth ... Chairman-elect
Jennifer Hilliard .... Testing Chairman
Margaret Null Braselton ...... Testing Co-Chairman

1995-1996

Kimberly Davis Stockseth ... Chairman
Jennifer Hilliard .... Chairman-elect
Katy Haden Einspanier .... Marketing Director

1996-1997

Sherri Todd Anderson .... Chairman
Michelle Germano .... Chairman-elect

Committee Members 1994-1996

Martha Lewis
Laura D. Moore
Amy Taylor
Pat Eldridge
Jane Dodson

Lisa Roberson
Katy Haden Einspanier
Cindy Wintermute
Jenifer Miller
Nancy Newton
Kathy Hayes

Sustaining Advisors 1994-1996

Janey Davy Cone
Kathy Jones Davies
Carol Anne Theis Davis
Mary Beth Delano
Claire Essing
Lynn Mahaffey
Carroll Patton Matthews

Lucy McCracken
Ella Wall Prichard
Helen Scibienski Swetman
Daryl Hause Tanner
Marcie Taylor
Mary Sue Ogg Wisdom

Community Advisors

Claudia Blucher Harrell
Martha Kiel

Presidents-Junior League of Corpus Christi, Inc.

Susie Walker-Atchison 1993-1994
Mary Beth Delano 1994-1995
Claire Samo 1995-1996
Jennifer Munroe Skrobarczyk 1997-1998

7

¡VIVA! Favorites

Appetizers

Military Presence

South Texas has a long history with the military, in part, leading to the prosperity of the region. Corpus Christi itself has seen battle during the Civil War, the city was first shelled in 1862, and in World War I. The Nueces River made a good camp site for military forts and in 1845 General Zachery Taylor landed with fifteen hundred troops to establish a federal post in Texas. This was the beginning, when the area became recognized as a strategic place for military operations. Following the prosperity of Taylor's army forces the settlers started to stream in as well. At the time, the Coastal Bend was known as the "Naples of the Gulf", due to its almost tropical climate and the availability of hunting and fishing. Later, the national military branches took advantage of its proximity to Mexico, its vast expanses and its seaports. During the 1940's, South Texas and the modern military formed partnerships that have endured. A few of these installations still thrive with thousands of enlisted and civilian employees. Naval Station Corpus Christi, Naval station Kingsville and Naval Station Ingleside have been recognized as vital training grounds for advanced troops and as centers of mine warfare training. Due to military history and area's amenities, thousands of military personnel retire in South Texas. They're not the only ones. A former aircraft carrier, the USS Lexington is now the Lexington Museum and is moored in drydock on North Beach. Upon dedication in 1992, "The Blue Ghost" had served longer and set more records than any other aircraft carrier in naval history. Commissioned in 1943, the carrier participated in nearly every operation in the Pacific Theater during twenty-one months of combat in World War II. The brig, military quarters, engine and boiler rooms are open for inspection. And on its flightdeck and hangar bays, rest various military aircraft that tell some of the history of the United States military. In 1996, Naval Station Ingleside became the new homeport for the USS Inchon, a command control and support ship for the Navy's mine warfare force.

Watermelon Pico de Gallo

1   jalapeño, seeded and
    minced
½   red onion, diced
1   cup cubed watermelon,
    seeded
1   cup cubed cantaloupe

1   cup cubed honeydew
1   cup cubed orange
    segments
2   tablespoons chopped
    cilantro
½   cup fresh lime juice

Toss all ingredients together and refrigerate 2 to 4 hours. Serve with tortilla chips as a dip or on a bed of lettuce surrounded with chips as a salad.

Yield: 5 cups

This dish can be served as a refreshing salad on a bed of lettuce. It will lighten up a Mexican dinner.

Salsa Fresca

1   large cucumber, peeled,
    seeded and chopped
2   large tomatoes, diced
½   medium onion, diced
2   jalapeños, seeded and
    minced

2   cloves garlic, minced
¼   cup chopped cilantro
1   teaspoon sugar
2   tablespoons oil
¼   cup lime juice

Combine all ingredients in a bowl. Toss well. Season with salt and pepper. Cover and refrigerate for at least 2 hours. Serve with tortilla or corn chips.

Keeps in the refrigerator for 1 week.

Yield: 3 cups

The seeds of jalapeño peppers contain the heat. The amount left in a dish determines how hot the dish will be.

Pronto Picante

1   (28-ounce) can diced
    tomatoes
3-4 jalapeños, seeded and
    diced

1   clove garlic, minced
1   small onion, diced
1   teaspoon salt

Drain juice from tomatoes and place juice in blender. Add jalapeño, garlic, and salt to blender, pulse. Add tomatoes and pulse again. Refrigerate and serve with chips.

Yield: 2 cups

Homemade salsa makes a great gift. Place in sterilized jars and store in refrigerator, or process in a hot water bath.

Salsa Verde

3	medium green tomatoes, chopped	3	medium ripe avocados, diced
4	tomatillos, chopped	1	tablespoon cilantro
1	jalapeño, seeded	1	teaspoon salt
2	cloves garlic, chopped	1½	cups sour cream

Bring 2 cups water to a boil. Place green tomatoes, tomatillos, jalapeño, and garlic in pot, reduce heat, and simmer until tomatoes are soft. Remove from heat, drain and cool completely. Place ½ avocado and ½ tomato mixture in a blender and blend until smooth. Pour into bowl and repeat with the other half avocado and tomato mixture. Fold in sour cream and salt, and stir well. Chill for several hours. Serve as a dip with tortilla chips or as a topping for chicken enchiladas.

Yield: 5 to 6 cups

This wonderful, creamy dip is a perfect match with red salsa.

Black Bean Salsa

2	(15-ounce) cans black beans, rinsed and drained	¼	cup chopped cilantro
		2	cloves garlic, minced
1	(14-ounce) can whole kernel corn, drained	4	tablespoons lime juice
2	large tomatoes, seeded and chopped	2	tablespoons olive oil
		2	tablespoons red wine vinegar
1	large avocado, chopped	1	teaspoon salt
1	jalapeño, seeded and minced	½	teaspoon black pepper

Combine all ingredients in a large bowl. Cover and chill 1 hour. Garnish with fresh cilantro. Serve with tortilla chips.

Substitute parsley if fresh cilantro is not available.

Yield: 6 cups

Can also be served over a bed of lettuce as a salad.

Kiko's Pico de Gallo

1   medium onion, chopped
3   fresh firm tomatoes,
    chopped
1   large clove garlic,
    crushed

3   serrano peppers, minced
juice of 1 lemon
1   cup chopped cilantro
salt to taste

Mix all ingredients and refrigerate. Keep cold and serve as soon as possible.

Onions should be firm and crispy when pico is served.

Yield: 6 to 8 servings

Turn this basic pico recipe into Pico Avocado by adding 1 diced avocado.

Cowboy Caviar

1   (15-ounce) can hominy,
    drained
1   (15-ounce) can black-
    eyed peas, drained
2   medium tomatoes,
    chopped

1   bell pepper, finely
    chopped
½   cup finely chopped onion
2   green onions, chopped
¼   cup chopped fresh
    cilantro
1   cup picante sauce

Combine all ingredients and chill. Serve with tortilla chips.

Yield: 6 to 8 servings

Cilantro is the fresh leaves of the coriander plant used in cooking and as a garnish.

Gazpacho Dip

1   (4-ounce) can chopped
    green chilies
1   (4-ounce) jar chopped
    black olives, drained
1   (14½-ounce) can diced
    tomatoes

5   green onions, chopped
1   tablespoon oil
3   tablespoons garlic
vinegar
garlic salt to taste

Mix all ingredients in bowl. Serve with corn or tortilla chips.

Yield: 3 cups

Chunky Guacamole

4	avocados, diced	1-2	serrano peppers, seeded
2	small tomatoes, diced		and minced
½	onion, minced	salt	
1	tablespoon lemon juice		

Combine first 5 ingredients, and toss gently. Season to taste with salt. Cover until ready to use.

To keep from turning brown, either seal surface of guacamole with plastic wrap or stir seeds in before refrigerating.

Yield: 2 cups

The traditional Mexican method of keeping guacamole from turning brown is to cover surface completely with milk. Pour off before serving.

Good Luck Dip

1¾	cups dried black eyed peas, sorted and washed	1	cup butter
5	cups water	2	cups grated sharp American cheese
5	whole pickled jalapeños, reserve liquid	1	(4-ounce) can chopped green chilies
⅓	cup chopped onion	1	tablespoon jalapeño liquid
1	clove garlic, chopped		

Canned peas can be used to save time. A great way to get the black eyed peas you need for luck the whole year long! Don't wait until New Year's to try this great dip.

Place peas in heavy saucepan, cover with water, bring to boil, and cook for 2 minutes. Remove from heat, cover, and soak for 1 hour. Drain. Combine peas with 5 cups water and bring to boil. Reduce heat, cover, and simmer 1 hour or until tender. Drain. Combine peas, jalapeño, onion, and garlic in food processor and blend until smooth. Set aside. Combine butter and cheese in top of double boiler. Cook over boiling water until melted. Add jalapeño liquid and pea mixture. Stir well. Serve with corn chips.

Vegetable Ginger Dip

1   cup mayonnaise
1   (8-ounce) container sour cream
1   (8-ounce) can water chestnuts, drained and chopped
¼   cup grated onion
3   tablespoons crystallized ginger
1   clove garlic, minced
1   tablespoon soy sauce
dash of hot sauce

Mix all ingredients, cover, and chill at least 8 hours. Serve with fresh vegetables or crackers.

Yield: 10 servings

Bean Dip

1 can refried beans
1 pint sour cream
1 cup picante sauce

Combine all ingredients until smooth. Serve warm or cold with chips.

Cajun Queso

2   pounds Velveeta
1   (8-ounce) can tomatoes with chilies, diced
1   pound pork sausage (regular or hot)
1   bunch green onions, chopped
3   stalks celery, chopped
1   small bell pepper, chopped
1   tablespoon Italian seasoning or any fresh herbs

Brown sausage. Drain, reserving 2 tablespoons grease. Sauté onion, celery, and pepper in reserved grease until soft. In a double boiler, melt cheese. Add tomatoes, sausage, and vegetables to cheese and mix well. Add seasoning and serve warm in a chafing dish with tortilla or corn chips.

Can be made ahead and reheated. Add chopped jalapeños, garlic, and picante sauce to make it spicier.

Yield: 20 servings, as a dip

In place of a double boiler, cheese can be melted over low heat stirring constantly or microwave oven at 50% power stirring every few minutes.

Devil Dip

1	(6-ounce) package chive cream cheese, softened	¼	teaspoon salt
2	tablespoons mayonnaise	⅛	teaspoon black pepper
1	teaspoon mustard	2	hard-boiled eggs, chopped
½	teaspoon Worcestershire sauce	3	tablespoons milk

Combine all ingredients and chill. Serve with crackers.
Sprinkle with paprika for color.

Yield: 1 cup

Manly Man Dip

1 pound Velveeta cheese
2 cups Miracle Whip
1 (6-ounce) can chopped jalapeño peppers, reserve liquid
½ onion, chopped

Melt cheese over low heat in a heavy sauce-pan. Add remaining ingredients. Stir well. Serve with corn or tortilla chips. Hot and oh so spicy!

Shrimp Queso

½	cup evaporated milk	1	cup picante sauce
8	ounces grated sharp Cheddar cheese	2	cups shrimp, cooked and chopped
8	ounces grated Monterey Jack cheese		

Heat milk in top of double boiler, add cheeses and stir until melted. Add picante and shrimp, mix well. Serve warm with tortilla chips.

Yield: 8 servings

Shrimp and Artichoke Dip

2	cups sour cream	1½	cups shrimp, cooked and cleaned
1	cup mayonnaise	2	(6-ounce) jars marinated artichoke hearts, drained
1	tablespoon capers		
2	tablespoons grated onion		
1	tablespoon horseradish		

Combine sour cream and next 4 ingredients. Chop shrimp and artichokes in small pieces. Add to sauce and refrigerate overnight. Serve cold with crackers or chips.

Yield: 6 cups

Kitchen Sink Queso

1½ pounds ground meat
1   small onion, chopped
2   pounds Velveeta cheese
1   (10-ounce) package
    frozen chopped broccoli,
    thawed
1   (8-ounce) can
    mushrooms, drained
1   (8-ounce) can tomatoes
    with chilies

Brown meat with onion and drain. Melt cheese over low heat. Add meat and remaining ingredients, heat thoroughly. Serve hot.

Great over baked potato, hot dogs, or scrambled eggs.

Yield: 20 dip servings

Chicken and Mushroom Quesadillas

½ pound mushrooms,
   sliced
2 tablespoons butter
1 cup cooked, shredded
   chicken
¼ cup chicken broth
   salt and pepper
8 flour tortillas
2 cups grated Monterey
   Jack cheese
½ cup picante sauce

Sauté mushrooms in butter until soft. Add chicken and broth, simmer 2 to 3 minutes. Season to taste with salt and pepper. Sprinkle ¼ cup cheese on half of each tortilla. Top cheese with 1 tablespoon picante sauce. Sprinkle even amount of chicken mixture on each tortilla and fold to form a half moon. Grill on greased griddle or skillet until slightly brown and crusty. Slice in pie wedges and serve with picante sauce, guacamole, and sour cream.

Yield: 8 servings

Stuffed quesadillas look like turnovers. All have cheese in common, are crisp on the outside, and a warm center. These moon-shaped pockets can be stuffed with the best your refrigerator and imagination will allow. A Tex-Mex delight!

Vegetable Nachos with Cilantro Cream

Mexican Pizza

  flour tortillas
  refried beans
  picante sauce
  grated cheese
  diced green chilies
  diced onions
  diced tomatoes

Spread beans over tortillas. Top with picante and other toppings. Place on cookie sheet and bake.

½ cup sour cream
2 tablespoons chopped cilantro
1 cup zucchini, quartered lengthwise and sliced thin
½ cup shredded carrot
⅓ cup sliced green onion
1½ teaspoons ground cumin
4 teaspoons cooking oil
1 (15-ounce) can refried beans
4 cups tortilla chips
1 (4-ounce) can diced green chilies or
2 jalapeño, seeded and chopped
1 cup grated Cheddar cheese
½ cup chopped and seeded tomato
¼ cup sliced black olives

To make cilantro cream: stir together sour cream and cilantro in small bowl. Cover and set aside. Sauté zucchini, carrot, onion, and cumin in oil for 3 to 4 minutes or until vegetables are crisp tender. Spread beans on each chip and place on cookie sheet in single layer. Spoon vegetable mixture over chips and sprinkle with chilies and cheese. Broil 4 to 6 minutes, watching closely. To serve, carefully transfer chips to a platter, top with dollops of cilantro cream and sprinkle with tomatoes and olives.

Yield: 8 servings

Papa George's Barbecued Shrimp

24 jumbo shrimp, peeled and deveined
1 (2-ounce) can anchovies
12 slices bacon, cut in half
skewers or toothpicks

Lay small piece of anchovy along back of shrimp, wrap with ½ piece of bacon, and thread onto skewer or secure with toothpick. Grill over medium fire until bright pink and bacon is cooked.

May also be cooked under a broiler.

Yield: 12 servings

Ceviche

3	pounds fillet of fish, cubed (redfish, trout, or any firm white fish)	2	cups chopped onion
20	limes, juiced (about 2 cups) and divided	1	cup chopped cilantro
4	cups chopped tomatoes	1	whole jalapeño, chopped (or more to taste)
			salt to taste

Place cubed fish in a shallow glass pan. Pour lime juice over, making sure each piece is submerged; marinate in refrigerator 6 hours or overnight. Drain and discard marinade. In large bowl, combine fish, tomato, onion, cilantro, and jalapeño. Add juice of 5 limes and salt to taste.

Serve as an appetizer with tortilla chips.

Yield: 12 servings

Corpus Christi is the heart of the Texas fishing industry. Party fishing boats and commercial shrimp boats dock in the downtown area and offer fresh seafood daily.

Shrimp Quesadillas

4	ounces shrimp, boiled and peeled	2	ounces Pepper Jack cheese, grated
¼	teaspoon ground cumin	4	flour tortillas
2	ounces Monterey Jack cheese, grated		guacamole
			pico de gallo
			sour cream

Cut shrimp into ½ inch pieces, sprinkle with ground cumin and set aside. Sprinkle Monterey Jack cheese on one flour tortilla, top with shrimp, sprinkle with pepper jack cheese, and top with another flour tortilla. On a hot pan or griddle, heat one side of tortilla until cheese is melted and shrimp is warm. Flip and brown other side. Cut into 6 pie wedges. Serve with side dishes of guacamole, pico de gallo, and sour cream.

Can assemble a few hours ahead, cover, and refrigerate until ready to cook.

Yield: 4 appetizer servings

From Water Street Oyster Bar, a favorite restaurant of locals and visitors.

Oysters Caliente

6	freshly shucked oysters
¼	cup picante sauce

¼	cup grated Monterey Jack cheese
6	slices pickled jalapeños

Wash oysters, reserving bottom half of shell. Place the oyster on the shell, cover with picante sauce and cheese. Bake at 400° for 7 to 10 minutes until cheese is melted and oyster is hot. Remove from oven and garnish with a slice of jalapeño.

Best served piping hot from the oven.

Yield: 1 to 2 servings

A favorite from Water Street Oyster Bar and Seafood Company in Corpus Christi.

Dill Shrimp

3	pounds medium-size shrimp, peeled and deveined
	juice of 1 lemon
1	teaspoon salt
1	cup Miracle Whip
¼	cup sugar
¼	teaspoon salt

1	large red onion, sliced thin and separated into rings
⅓	cup fresh lemon juice
½	cup sour cream
2	tablespoons dried dill weed

Corpus Christi is the sixth largest port in the United States. The port provides over 38,000 jobs for the community.

Bring 3-quarts water to a boil. Add shrimp, lemon juice, and salt. When water returns to a boil, cook 3 to 4 minutes, until shrimp turn pink. Drain and cover with ice to stop the cooking process. Combine remaining ingredients in large mixing bowl with tight fitting lid. Add shrimp and toss. Refrigerate, covered, overnight to marry flavors. Toss before serving.

Yield: 12 servings

Water Street Oysters

12	freshly shucked oysters	¼	cup grated Monterey Jack cheese
⅓	cup cocktail sauce		
¼	cup grated Cheddar cheese	6	tablespoons cooked and crumbled bacon

Wash oysters, reserving bottom shell. Place the oyster on shell and top with cocktail sauce and cheeses. Bake at 400° for 7 to 10 minutes, until cheese is melted and oyster is hot. Remove from oven and sprinkle with bacon.

Yield: 2 to 3 servings

Smoked Salmon Cheesecake

½	cup Parmesan cheese	1	tablespoon fresh dill weed
½	cup rye cracker crumbs		
1⅓	pounds cream cheese	1	pinch cayenne pepper
4	eggs	1	onion, finely chopped
7	ounces blue or Gorgonzola cheese	5	ounces smoked salmon, chopped fine
⅓	cup whipping cream		

Blend Parmesan cheese and cracker crumbs and pat into bottom of a greased 8-inch springform pan. Bake at 350° for 10 minutes. In a food processor, blend next 6 ingredients until smooth. Fold in onion and salmon. Pour in prepared crust and place in another pan containing hot water that reaches halfway up the sides. Bake at 350° for 1 hour and 20 minutes. Turn off oven and leave door ajar for 1 hour.

Should be prepared 1 day in advance so flavors can marry.

Smoked salmon, also known as "nova", refers to any form of smoked salmon regardless of its source.

Apricot Brie en Croûte

1	package frozen puff pastry (2 sheets), thawed	2	tablespoons apricot preserves
		1½	pound round Brie cheese

On waxed paper, roll out pastry large enough to cover cheese completely. Spread preserves in middle of dough and place cheese over preserves. Fold pastry up sides and over top, sealing edges. Place seam side down on baking sheet. Bake at 400° for 10 minutes. Reduce temperature to 325° for 20 minutes longer or until golden brown. Let stand at room temperature for 30 minutes before serving. Serve with crackers and fresh fruit.

Cut leftover dough in interesting shapes and decorate top of pastry before baking.

Yield: serves 12 to 18

Splendidly elegant served with a slightly dry Texas wine.

Goat Cheese and Sundried Tomato Torta

1	(8-ounce) package cream cheese, softened	1	cup basil pesto
12	ounces Montrachet goat cheese	1	(7-ounce) jar oil packed sundried tomatoes, drained and minced
1	cup unsalted butter, softened		

Line 8x1½-inch round cake pan with a double thickness of dampened cheesecloth, leaving enough to fold over top; set aside. Beat cheeses and butter until fluffy. Spoon ⅓ mixture in prepared cake pan covering bottom evenly. Spoon ½ pesto onto cheese layer. Repeat layers, ending with cheese. Cover with plastic wrap, then fold ends of cheesecloth over. Refrigerate at least 1 hour. Remove from refrigerator, fold back cheesecloth, and remove plastic wrap. Invert torte on plate. Top with tomatoes and serve with crackers.

Yield: 15 to 20 servings

Cucumber Rounds with Salmon Mousse

2	medium cucumbers, peeled and sliced ½-inch thick	5	ounces cream cheese
		3	ounces sour cream
3	ounces smoked salmon	1	teaspoon fresh dill weed
		½	teaspoon lemon pepper

Scoop out small well in middle of each cucumber slice. Place remaining ingredients in a food processor. Process until smooth. Place mixture in a pastry bag and pipe into each cucumber round. Sprinkle with paprika or spice of your choice.

Yield: 8 to 10 servings

This is a simple, yet elegant, appetizer contributed by Christian Chavanne, chef at the Corpus Christi Yacht Club.

Mushroom Provolone Pinwheels

1	package frozen puff pastry (2 sheets), thawed	2	tablespoons Worcestershire sauce
1	pound mushrooms, finely chopped	2	tablespoons soy sauce
2	tablespoons butter	1	tablespoon hot sauce
4	cloves garlic, minced	8	ounces Provolone cheese, sliced thin
¼	cup chopped onions	1	egg, beaten
		2	tablespoons garlic salt

Unfold pastry on lightly floured surface and set aside. Sauté mushrooms, garlic, and onions in butter until all moisture has evaporated. Add Worcestershire, soy, and hot sauce and sauté until liquid is absorbed, about 5 minutes. Layer cheese over pastry sheets and sprinkle mushrooms over cheese. Starting with long end, roll up jelly roll fashion, and slice in ½-inch rounds. Brush with egg and sprinkle with garlic salt. Place on greased baking sheet and bake at 400° for 15 minutes.

If dough is too soft to slice, wrap in wax paper and freeze for 1 hour.

Yield: 40 pinwheels

Mexican Flag

1 (8-ounce)package cream cheese, softened
1 cup picante sauce
1 avocado, diced

Place cream cheese on a serving dish. Cover with picante and avocado in rows similar to the Mexican flag. Serve with chips or crackers.

Florentine Crescents

2	(8-ounce) packages refrigerated crescent rolls	16-24	spinach leaves, washed and stemmed
1	(8-ounce) package herb cream cheese, softened		

Preheat oven to 350°. Unroll dough into 4 long rectangles and press perforations together. Spread cream cheese onto rectangles to within ¼ inch of edges. Lay spinach over cheese. Starting at short end, roll up rectangle and press edges to seal. Chill if dough becomes too soft. Cut each rectangle into 8 slices and place on ungreased cookie sheet. Bake 12 to 18 minutes or until golden brown. Serve warm.

Yield: 32 crescents

Pizza Pinwheels

1	package frozen puff pastry (2 sheets), thawed	1	(4-ounce)package pepperoni slices
8	ounces Mozzarella cheese, grated	1	egg, beaten
½	cup pizza sauce	¼	cup Parmesan cheese

Lay puff pastry sheets over a lightly floured surface and spread pizza sauce evenly over both sheets. Sprinkle with cheese and spread pepperoni slices over top. Starting at long end, roll up jelly roll fashion and cut in 2-inch slices. Place on greased baking sheet and brush with egg. Top with Parmesan cheese and bake at 400° for 15 minutes.

If dough is too soft to slice, wrap in wax paper and freeze for 1 hour.

Yield: 24 pinwheels

Garlic Cream and Pesto Torta

Pesto
2 cloves garlic, chopped
1 cup chopped fresh basil
1 cup Parmesan cheese

½ cup olive oil
¼ cup pine nuts

Garlic Cream
1 (8-ounce) package cream
   cheese, softened
¼ cup butter, softened

2-3 cloves garlic, minced
½ cup shelled pistachios,
   chopped

Torta
1 pound Provolone cheese,
   sliced thin

½ cup sundried tomatoes,
   drained and chopped

For pesto: process all pesto ingredients until paste is formed. For garlic cream; blend cheese, butter, and garlic well. Add pistachios. To assemble: line a loaf pan with damp cheesecloth with excess hanging over sides. Line pan with ½ of Provolone, overlapping to cover bottom and sides of pan. Divide remaining cheese into 3 equal portions. Spread ½ pesto over cheese in pan. Add a layer of Provolone and ½ of the tomatoes. Carefully spread all garlic cream and top with remaining tomatoes. Next layer Provolone, remaining pesto and top with last of cheese. Fold cheesecloth over loaf and press firmly. Refrigerate at least 3 hours. To serve: fold cloth back, invert on serving plate, and ease out of pan. Serve with crackers or crusty French bread.

Can be made 3 days before serving.

Yield: 25 servings

From its very beginning, Corpus Christi was a military town. It started as a trading post and fort that welcomed and hosted half of the existing United States Army in 1845. The military remains the largest single employer in the city.

Olive Bites

1 (8-ounce) package cream
   cheese, softened
Dash of salt
Dash of white pepper
Dash of garlic powder

1 (8-ounce) jar stuffed
   green olives, drained on
   paper towel
1 cup finely ground pecans

Combine cheese and spices. Form cheese mixture around each olive, covering completely. Roll in pecan meal and refrigerate. Slice in 2 to 3 pieces and serve.

This is a fun appetizer for the Christmas holidays.

Yield: 48 bites

Olive Cheese Garlic Bread

2	cups mayonnaise	1	(4-ounce) can black olives, chopped
3	small cloves garlic, chopped	1	(4-ounce) jar green olives, drained, rinsed and chopped
4	ounces Parmesan cheese		
3	green onions, chopped	1	loaf French bread, sliced
4	ounces mild Cheddar cheese, grated		

Combine all the above ingredients together except bread and refrigerate, up to 24 hours. Spread on sliced bread and bake at 375° until mixture is melted and bread is brown, about 10 minutes. Serve immediately.

Cocktail rye or pumpernickel works well, too.

Yield: 10 to 12 servings

Onion Melt

1 cup onion, minced
1 cup mayonnaise
1 cup grated Cheddar cheese
paprika

Mix all ingredients, except paprika, and place in a small baking dish. Sprinkle with paprika and bake at 350° for 30 minutes. Allow to cool 10 minutes before serving. Serve with crackers or chips.

Toasted Parmesan Canapés

5	tablespoons Parmesan cheese	1	small onion, minced
1	cup mayonnaise	1	loaf thin white bread

Remove crust from bread and quarter slices. Mix mayonnaise and Parmesan cheese and spread on bread squares. Sprinkle with onions and more Parmesan cheese. Broil until golden brown. Serve immediately.

Bread may be cut in various shapes with cookie cutter before spreading with mayonnaise/cheese mixture.

Yield: 20 servings

Buffalo Chicken Strips

1	cup soy sauce	¼	cup Louisiana style hot sauce
½	cup sugar		
¼	cup oil	4	pounds chicken strips, cleaned
½	cup pineapple juice		
3	cloves garlic, chopped		

Combine first 6 ingredients. Place chicken in marinade and refrigerate 24 hours. Drain and discard marinade. Arrange in single layer on cookie sheet and bake at 350° for 1 hour.

Serve on wooden skewers with pineapple chunks on the end.

¡VIVA! Tradiciones

Sesame-Parmesan Toasts

1 loaf very thinly sliced white bread, crusts removed	½ cup sesame seeds
1 cup butter, softened	1 teaspoon seasoned salt
1 cup Parmesan cheese	¼ teaspoon cayenne pepper

Preheat oven to 350°. Cut bread slices in half diagonally. Combine remaining ingredients and spread generously on bread, covering completely. Place on cookie sheets. Reduce oven temperature to 250° and bake for about 1 hour until bread is completely dry and crisp. Cool on racks. Can be made ahead and stored in tins.

This is delicious in place of chips or crackers with cold buffets, or with soups and salads.

Yield: 40 to 50 toasts

The Whitehall Club in Chicago had baskets of these on the dining tables. They will continue to crisp after baking, but must be thoroughly dried out in the oven.

Tex-Mex Won Tons

½ pound ground beef	1 tablespoon ketchup
¼ cup chopped onion	1½ teaspoons chili powder
2 tablespoons chopped bell pepper	¼ teaspoon ground cumin
½ of a (15-ounce) can refried beans	4 dozen won ton skins cooking oil for deep frying taco sauce
¼ cup grated Cheddar cheese	

Brown ground beef with onion and bell pepper. Drain. Add beans, next 4 ingredients, and mix well. Place won ton skin with one point toward you. Spoon generous teaspoon of meat mixture on center of skin. Fold bottom point of skin over filling and tuck point under filling. Fold side corners over, forming an envelope shape. Roll toward remaining corner, moisten point, and press to seal. Repeat with remaining won ton skins and filling. Fry a few at a time in hot oil, about 1 minute per side. Use slotted spoon to remove won tons. Drain on paper towels. Serve warm with taco sauce.

Leftovers can be frozen. Reheat, loosely covered, in a 350° oven for 10 to 12 minutes.

Yield: 48 won tons

Mexican Folklore: If you feel some kind of harm is going to happen to you, sprinkle your shoe with red pepper to ward off all evil.

Armadillo Eggs

¾	pound Monterey Jack cheese, (½ pound grated, ¼ pound sliced)	15	canned whole jalapeños
½	pound ground sausage	2	eggs, well beaten with 1 tablespoon water
1½	cups Bisquick	2	envelopes Shake and Bake for Pork

If armadillo's did lay eggs, they would certainly look like these spicy appetizers. These don't bite but they do kick!

Combine grated cheese, sausage, and Bisquick. Knead and set aside. Slit and seed jalapeños. Stuff each with a sliver of cheese. Pinch off small piece of dough and make a ¼-inch thick pancake. Wrap completely around jalapeño, sealing edges. Mold into egg shape. Coat each egg in Shake and Bake. Dip into beaten egg mixture and roll again in Shake and Bake, coating the egg well. Bake on ungreased cookie sheet at 325° for 20 to 30 minutes, until cheese bubbles. Turn 2 to 3 times. Serve warm with picante sauce.

May be frozen and cooked at a later time.

Yield: 15 servings

Marinated Cheese

16	ounces Mozzarella cheese	1	tablespoon cayenne pepper
2	cups olive oil	1	tablespoon oregano
1	medium bell pepper, cut in strips	1	teaspoon crushed red pepper
¼	cup wine vinegar	1	teaspoon thyme
		2	cloves garlic, halved

A great gift!

Cut cheese into ½-inch cubes. Prick cheese with fork and place in 1-quart container. In saucepan, heat remaining ingredients. Cool and pour over cheese. Store in refrigerator for 2 weeks. Before serving, let stand at room temperature for 1 hour. Serve in salads, antipasto, or relish trays.

Stores in refrigerator for 6 weeks.

Yield: 3 cups

Beverages

Sailing

S ailing is often an intrinsic part of life on the coast and it can be one of the seashore's most beautiful sports to watch. Of course, a long sailing trip is the favorite weekend activity for many. Some can't wait that long. In the middle of the week, the Wednesday night sailboat regatta races offer the avid sailor a night of friendly competition around Corpus Christi Bay. Early in the evening as skippers and their crews hoist sails and ready for the races and as the water around the marina become dotted with boats, residents and visitors crowd restaurants and walk the seawall for views of this awesome spectacle. Groups strolling along the bayfront stop to admire the view. As night falls, the sun sets in reds, yellows and blues, the tall white sails linger across the shadowed and light flickering waves. During the winter months and especially the holiday season, the docked boats put on a show of a different sort, Harbor Lights. With strands of white and colored illuminations strung up their masts, the whole marina is transformed into a wondrous display of light twinkling over the waters. The usual southeast wind often causes the waters to be a bit choppy and can be intimidating for the beginner to learn the complicated strategies of sailing. But the rewards of feeling the strength of the wind against your arms and becoming one with the sea far out weigh any fears or intimidations. Boats and yachts of all kinds are docked here and sailors from all over make stops here. Corpus Christi Bay has also been the sight of various professional competitions in recent years, including the North American 470 Championships and the Finn National Championships, that are a preamble for the United States Olympic Trials. For residents who like to spend their weekends on the Gulf waters, there is the annual Harvest Moon Regatta, which routes sailors 150 miles from Galveston to Port Aransas, the longest port-to-port offshore race in the country. The Ruff Rider lures sailors from several states for a two-day cruise on their catamaran, trimarian, monohulls or even sailboats from South Padre Island to John F. Kennedy Causeway. Any sailor who wants to go back in time can learn to sail aboard Christopher Columbus' Niña, moored in Corpus Christi Bay.

Fackenthal Margaritas

1	quart gold tequila	8	(6-ounce) cans frozen
1	quart Cointreau		limeade
1	pint Triple Sec		

Mix all ingredients in large container to form base. Fill blender with ice, pour in 1 cup base mixture and blend until smooth.
Base will keep in freezer for months.
Yield: Base for 60 drinks

Poco Loco Smashes

1	cup rum	2	cups orange juice
1	cup coconut rum	2	cups pineapple juice
1	cup apricot liquor		

Combine all ingredients and pour into glasses filled with crushed ice.
Yield: 7 cups

This drink comes from one of our many "Beach to Bay" teams. It will help you forget about sore muscles. The Beach to Bay is the largest relay marathon in the United States, which attracts runners from all over the country. Over 6,000 participants run from the beach on North Padre Island to Corpus Christi Bay.

Casa Cabeza Margaritas

1	(6-ounce) can frozen limeade	1	shot bar syrup -or- Mexican Jarable
1	can tequila		
1/3	can Gran Marnier		

Place all ingredients in blender and fill with ice. Blend until smooth.
Use the empty limeade can for measuring.
Yield: 4 servings

Guests will always leave smiling after 2 of these!

Bellinis

2	cups white wine		3	(12-ounce) cans peach
2	cups champagne			nectar
1	cup peach Schnapps		1	cup rum
			½	cup powdered sugar

Combine all ingredients until sugar is dissolved. Place in freezer overnight. Remove from freezer and stir. Mixture should be slushy.

Yield: 10 drinks

The first Bellini was served at Harry's Bar in Venice, Italy.

La Mota Lizard

1	(6-ounce) can frozen lemonade		12	ounces gin
			10	fresh mint leaves
juice of 1 lime				

This will make a summer night fly by!

Place all ingredients in blender and fill with ice. Blend until smooth and enjoy.

Use the empty lemonade can for measuring.

Yield: 4 drinks

Big Daddy's Planter's Punch

1	(6-ounce) can pineapple juice		6	ounces rum
				dash of bitters
1	(6-ounce) can orange juice			dash of grenadine, for red color

A potent potion!

Place all ingredients in a blender with a handful of ice. Blend until smooth. Pour in tall glasses filled with ice.

Yield: 4 to 6 drinks

Jose Antonio's Sangria

1 (4-liter) bottle Burgundy
wine
3 apples, diced
3 bananas, sliced
3 peaches, sliced
3 oranges, sliced
1 cup chopped watermelon
2 lemons, juiced
1 lemon, sliced
¼ cup sugar
1 teaspoon cinnamon

In a very large container, place cut fruits in wine. Add lemon juice, sugar and cinnamon. Stir gently. Refrigerate several hours.

Pour Burgundy over fruit as it runs low.

Yield: 40 drinks

The Padre Island National Seashore located south of Corpus Christi is part of a 60-mile stretch of Texas shoreline and is the largest undeveloped barrier island in the continental United States.

Killer Coffee

1 shot brandy
1 shot orange Curaçao
1 shot Kahlúa
2 cups fresh brewed coffee
whipped cream

Mix alcohols and divide between 2 coffee cups. Fill with fresh brewed coffee and top with whipped cream.

Yield: 2 drinks

Red Hot Tea Mix

1 (9-ounce) jar Tang
2 cups sugar
1 cup instant tea
6 ounces instant lemonade
1 teaspoon cinnamon
½ teaspoon ground cloves
½ cup red hots candy

Mix all ingredients together and store in a sealed container. Place 3 heaping teaspoons in a mug. Add 1 cup boiling water and stir.

Wrap in colorful paper, tie with cinnamon sticks, and tuck in a beautiful coffee mug.

Strawberry Banana Slush Punch

4	cups sugar	4	bananas
6	cups water	1	(16-ounce) package
1	(46-ounce) can pineapple		frozen strawberries
	juice	½	cup lemon juice
1	(46-ounce) can orange	5	quarts ginger ale, chilled
	juice		

Boil sugar and water in saucepan until sugar dissolves. Cool. Coarsely chop bananas and strawberries in food processor. Combine all ingredients, except ginger ale, in large container and freeze. When ready to serve, place frozen slush in punch bowl and pour ginger ale over.

Can freeze in decorative molds or rings.

Yield: 30 drinks

Bourbon Slush

2	cups strong brewed tea	7	cups water
1	(12-ounce) can frozen	1	cup sugar
	limeade	2½	cups bourbon
1	(12-ounce) can frozen	2	liters ginger ale
	orange juice		

Many party fishing boats operate out of Corpus Christi Bay. They depart daily taking passengers out to try their luck. Some guides will even bait your hook for you!

Mix all ingredients, except ginger ale, in large container and freeze. To serve, spoon frozen mixture into glasses and add equal amount of ginger ale.

Yield: 25 drinks

Fruit and Sherbet Punch

2	(6-ounce) cans frozen lemonade	1	quart cranberry juice cocktail
1	(6-ounce) can frozen limeade	2	(2-liter) bottles ginger ale
3	cans water	2	drops red food coloring, optional
1	(46-ounce) can pineapple juice	½	gallon orange sherbet

Combine juices, water, and ginger ale in large punch bowl. Just before serving scoop in sherbet.

Yield: 30 to 40 drinks

Mango Mimosa

1 *bottle champagne*
2 *(12-ounce) cans mango nectar*

Mix and serve chilled.

Favorite Hot Cocoa Mix

4	ounces cocoa	1	(9.6-ounce) box powdered milk
1	pound confectioners sugar	¼	teaspoon salt
6	ounces non-dairy coffee creamer	¼	teaspoon cinnamon
			marshmallows, optional

Sift ingredients together and add marshmallows , if desired. Store in sealed container. Place three heaping teaspoons in a mug, add boiling water. Stir with a cinnamon stick.

Adjust amount of cocoa to your taste.

A great family hot cocoa mix.

Beverly's Milk Punch

1   gallon quality vanilla
     ice cream, softened
2-3 cups bourbon

4   cups milk
     nutmeg

Mix ice cream with bourbon and milk. Taste and adjust alcohol content with more bourbon or more milk. Sprinkle with nutmeg.

Bourbon can be adjusted to individual preferences.

Breakfast

Windsurfers

Ocean Drive, in Corpus Christi, provides one of the best views in Coastal Bend. It is also one of the best places to witness a popular water sport in the area, windsurfing, as sailboards skim over the Gulf of Mexico waters. In fact, conditions are so good that the city is recognized as one of the premier locations in the country for recreational and competitive windsurfing. Consistent wind is the primary concern for any windsurfer, and Corpus Christi is among the windiest cities with an average annual wind speed of about 13 miles per hour. That is good for year-round surfing and sailing during the prime seasons in the spring and in the winter. Wind speeds may be 20 miles per hour for days in a row and the areas water conditions, which vary according to location, offer flat-water sailing for beginners to intermediate sailboarders, chop sailing for intermediate sailors, and ocean and wave sailing for the higher level seamen. Sites on the Laguna Madre, the lagoon between the barrier islands and the mainland, are good for flat-water boating. But the most popular sailboarding spots remain the parks along Ocean Drive, especially Oleander Point and Cole Park, both located on Corpus Christi Bay. The surf is usually small and choppy becoming choppier with increasing winds. On windy, choppy days, other boards and boats may stay off of the water, but the windsurfers take full advantage. Passers-by can marvel at the speed at which the boards fly, sometimes actually becoming airborne over the surf. It is the place to be for local sailboarders. The most advanced sailors may find a challenge during the winter months in Port Aransas whenever northern winds blow and waves grow to six feet tall or taller. Windsurfers from Mexico, Canada, and beyond often make the trek to sail on Corpus Christi's bay waters. Though there are plenty of chances for competition locally, the city has also been host to several international events, including the U.S. Open Sailboard Regatta and the International Boarding Association's North American Championship.

¡VIVA! Tradiciones

Pan Mañana

¼ cup butter
⅓ cup sugar
½ teaspoon cinnamon
1 teaspoon grated orange
   zest

⅔ cup orange juice juice
4 eggs, beaten
8 slices French bread
powdered sugar

Melt butter in shallow 3-quart casserole. Combine sugar, cinnamon, and zest and sprinkle over butter. In shallow bowl, mix juice and eggs. Dip bread into egg mixture and place in a single layer over butter and zest mixture. Pour remaining egg mixture over bread. Can be refrigerated overnight at this point. Bake uncovered at 325° for 25 minutes. Sprinkle with powdered sugar.

A tried and true goody for the guests of a cook who likes to sleep late.

Yield: 4 servings

Cream Cheese French Toast

8 slices bread
8 ounces cream cheese,
   softened
1 pint fresh strawberries,
   sliced

3 eggs, beaten
½ cup milk
1 teaspoon vanilla
2 tablespoons sugar
cinnamon

Spread 4 slices of bread with cream cheese. Lay strawberries over cream cheese and top with remaining bread. In shallow bowl, beat eggs with milk, vanilla and sugar. Dip each sandwich into egg mixture, coating both sides. Cook on hot griddle until brown, flip and cook other side. Sprinkle with cinnamon and extra strawberries. Serve warm with syrup.

This works well with fresh peaches too.

Yield: 4 servings

Banana Oat Pancakes

2	cups pancake mix, plain or whole wheat
2	cups milk
¾	cup oats
4	eggs, beaten
⅓	cup oil
½	cup raisins
2	bananas, sliced
	cinnamon

Combine first 5 ingredients in order listed, just until wet. Gently fold in raisins and bananas. Do not over mix. Cook on hot griddle until lightly brown, flip, and cook other side. Serve hot with honey, syrup, and jam.

Yield: 6 to 8 servings

Black Cherry Pancake

2	cups fresh or frozen pitted cherries
½	cup plus 2 tablespoons flour, divided
4	eggs, beaten
½	cup sugar
1¼	cups evaporated milk
1	teaspoon almond extract
2	teaspoons vanilla

A breakfast sweet from Christian Chavanne of the Corpus Christi Yacht Club.

Toss cherries with 2 tablespoons flour, set aside. Combine eggs, remaining flour, and sugar. Whisk in milk until free of lumps. Add almond extract and vanilla. Pour into greased 9-inch oven-proof skillet top with fruit. Bake at 350° for 45 minutes, until lightly brown and set. Cool 10 minutes. Serve hot or cold.

Yield: 6 servings

¡VIVA! Tradiciones

Crunchy Granola

3	cups regular oats	½	cup honey
1	cup grated coconut	¼	oil
½	cup coarsely chopped almonds	½	cup dried fruit (peaches, apricots, bananas, etc.)
½	cup raw sunflower seeds	½	cup raisins
½	cup unsweetened wheat germ		

In a large bowl, combine oats with next 4 ingredients. Combine honey and oil. Stir into dry mixture. Spread out on cookie sheet. Bake at 300° for 45 to 50 minutes, until light brown. Stir every 15 minutes. Remove from oven and cool. Toss in fruit and store in sealed container.

Eat as a snack or cereal.

Yield: 6½ cups

Gulf Coast Cheese Grits

1	cup quick grits, uncooked	6	ounces garlic cheese
6	tablespoons butter	1	teaspoon Tabasco
2	cups grated sharp Cheddar cheese	1	teaspoon Worcestershire
		1	teaspoon paprika

Cook grits according to package directions. Add butter and cheese and stir until melted. Add Tabasco and Worcestershire. Pour into greased 2-quart casserole; sprinkle with paprika. Bake at 350° for 30 minutes.

If garlic cheese is unavailable, substitute 6-ounces Velveeta and 2 teaspoons garlic powder.

Yield: 6 servings

Even if you hate grits, you'll love these.

Sorda Eggs Sardou

8	slices thin bread, quartered and toasted	½	pound ham, chopped
1	(14-ounce) can artichoke hearts, quartered	8	eggs
2	(10-ounce) boxes frozen chopped spinach, cooked and drained	½	cup milk or cream
		½	teaspoon salt
		½	teaspoon pepper
8	ounces cream cheese with chives, softened		Tabasco to taste
		3	tablespoons club soda
		1½	cups Hollandaise Sauce
			paprika

Hollandaise Sauce

4 egg yolks
2 teaspoons lemon
    juice
¼ teaspoon salt
dash of Tabasco
1 cup hot melted
    butter

Place first 4 ingredients in a blender and pulse. With motor running, slowly pour in butter.

Line a 9x13 buttered casserole with toast points. Scatter artichokes over toast. Combine spinach and cream cheese and spread over artichokes. Sprinkle ham over spinach. Beat eggs and next 3 ingredients in a bowl. Gently mix club soda with eggs. In non-stick skillet, scramble eggs until soft and still runny; spread over ham. Bake, covered at 350° for 35 minutes or until thoroughly heated. Uncover and cook 10 minutes more. Pour Hollandaise over and sprinkle with paprika.

Can be made as individual servings using English muffins in place of toast points.

Yield: 8 servings

Huevos Estrada

1½	pounds ham, chopped	1	pound sharp Cheddar cheese, grated
2	medium onions, chopped		
2	stalks celery, chopped	12	eggs, beaten
1	tablespoon butter	½	teaspoon dry mustard
8	slices bread, toasted, buttered and cubed	1½	teaspoons salt
		4	cups milk
			dash of Tabasco

A great "do ahead" for Sunday or holiday brunch.

In a non-stick skillet, sauté ham, onion, and celery in butter. In a large bowl, combine ham mixture with remaining ingredients. Pour in a 9x13 casserole. Bake at 350° for 1 hour or until set. For best results, assemble the night before, refrigerate and bake in the morning.

Yield: 8 to 10 servings

Chili Cheese Eggs

1	pound country style sausage	2	cups grated Monterey Jack cheese
12	eggs	1	cup cottage cheese
1	(4-ounce) can chopped green chilies	½	cup flour
2	cups grated sharp Cheddar cheese	1	teaspoon baking powder
		1	teaspoon salt
		½	cup butter, melted

Brown sausage in skillet, drain. In a large bowl, beat eggs well. Gradually add sausage and chilies. Add remaining ingredients and mix well. Pour in greased 9 x 13 casserole. Bake uncovered at 350° for 40 minutes. Let sit at least 20 minutes.

A little club soda in any scrambled eggs recipe results in a light fluffy dish.

Yield: 12 servings

There is not a defined recipe for Breakfast Tacos. They are simply a combination of eggs and whatever can be found in the refrigerator, such as potatoes, ham, sausage, bacon or beans. Scrambled together and wrapped in a flour tortilla with salsa.

Mushroom Cheese Strata

2	cups bread cubes, crusts removed	½	pound mushrooms, chopped
8	ounces Cheddar cheese, grated	3	eggs
½	pound bacon, fried crisp and crumbled	2	cups milk
¼	cup butter, melted	1	teaspoon prepared mustard
		¼	teaspoon salt

Place half of bread cubes in a buttered 1½-quart casserole. Layer half of cheese, bacon, and butter. Repeat layer and arrange mushrooms on top. Beat eggs and next 3 ingredients and pour over strata. Set casserole in another pan. Fill larger pan with water that reaches halfway up the sides. Bake uncovered at 300° for 90 minutes.

Ham or shrimp may be substituted for bacon.

Yield: 6 servings

This dish is best prepared in advance and refrigerated overnight before baking.

Migas

3	(6-inch) corn tortillas, cut in 1-inch pieces
3	tablespoons oil
½	cup chopped onion
½	cup chopped tomato
6	eggs
½	teaspoon salt
½	teaspoon pepper

Sauté tortilla strips in oil until almost crisp. Add onion and tomatoes; cook until tender. Add eggs, salt, and pepper and stir gently until eggs are set. Serve with salsa and a sprinkle of Cheddar cheese.

For a little zing, add 2 tablespoons chopped jalapeño.

Yield: 4 servings

Migas con Carne

Add ½ cup chorizo sausage to tortillas while frying.

Chicken Pecan Quiche

Crust

1	cup flour	½	teaspoon salt
½	cup grated sharp Cheddar cheese	¼	teaspoon paprika
¾	cup chopped pecans	⅓	cup oil

Filling

8	ounces cream cheese, softened	½	cup grated sharp Cheddar cheese
¼	cup mayonnaise	½	cup chicken broth
3	eggs, beaten	¼	cup minced onion
2	cups cooked cubed chicken	¼	teaspoon dried dill weed
		1	teaspoon Tabasco
		¼	teaspoon paprika

A ladies luncheon favorite.

Combine flour and next 5 crust ingredients until crumbly. Reserve ¼ of the mixture and press remaining crust in bottom and up sides of 9-inch pie pan. Bake at 350° for 10 minutes, cool. Mix cream cheese and mayonnaise until smooth. Add eggs and stir well. Add chicken and remaining ingredients; mix well. Pour into baked crust. Sprinkle with reserved crust crumbs and paprika. Bake at 325° for 45 minutes.

Yield: 6 to 8 servings

¡VIVA! Tradiciones

Spring Garden Pie

1	(9-inch) unbaked pie crust	4	large eggs	
2	small zucchini, scrubbed and grated	1½	cups heavy cream	
¼	cup Parmesan cheese	½	teaspoon salt	
4	ounces Gruyère cheese, grated	⅛	teaspoon nutmeg	
		⅛	teaspoon pepper	

Spread zucchini on paper towels and allow to drain for 20 to 30 minutes. Sprinkle cheese in pie shell; top with zucchini. Whisk eggs and next 4 ingredients until thoroughly blended. Pour mixture over zucchini. Bake at 375° for 45 minutes on center rack, until nicely browned and custard is set.

Experiment with your favorite combination of vegetables.

Yield: 4 to 6 servings

Crustless Ham Quiche

½	pound mushrooms	½	cup Parmesan cheese
2	tablespoons butter, melted	1	teaspoon onion powder
4	eggs	6	drops Tabasco
1	cup sour cream	2	cups grated Monterey Jack cheese
1	cup small curd cottage cheese	½	cup chopped cooked ham
¼	cup flour		

Sauté mushrooms in butter until soft. Drain and set aside. Combine eggs with next 6 ingredients in blender or food processor until thoroughly mixed. Combine mushrooms, egg mixture, cheese and ham. Pour in a greased quiche pan. Bake at 350° for 45 minutes or until puffed and golden brown. Cool 10 minutes before slicing.

Yield: 6 servings

Evaporated skim milk can be used in place of half and half in this recipe and most others.

Simple Sausage Quiche

½ pound hot sausage
5 eggs
1 cup whole kernel corn,
   drained

1 cup grated Cheddar
   cheese

Cook sausage in 8-inch oven-proof skillet until crumbly. Drain off grease. Combine eggs and corn. Pour over sausage without stirring. Place skillet in preheated 450° oven. Bake 10 to 15 minutes, until set. Sprinkle cheese over quiche and return to oven until cheese has melted. Cool several minutes before slicing.

Can easily be doubled using a 10-inch skillet and increasing cooking time.

Yield: 6 servings

Mother's Coffee Cake

Cake
1   cup butter
1¼ cups sugar
2   large eggs, beaten
1   cup sour cream

1   teaspoon vanilla
2   cups flour
1   teaspoon baking powder
½   teaspoon baking soda

Topping
1   cup chopped nuts
4   teaspoons sugar

2   teaspoons cinnamon

Cream butter and sugar. Add eggs, sour cream, and vanilla and beat well. Combine next 3 ingredients and slowly add to batter. Place half of batter in a greased 8-inch square pan. Combine topping ingredients and sprinkle half over batter. Pour in remaining batter and sprinkle with remaining topping. Bake at 350° for 50 minutes to 1 hour or until cake tests done.

Yield: 8 to 10 servings

Turkey Cranberry Cheesecake

Crust
1   (3-ounce) package stuffing mix, prepared to package directions, or use leftovers

Filling

2	tablespoons butter		salt and pepper
1	medium onion, chopped	2	tablespoons chopped chives
1	(16-ounce) container Ricotta cheese	1	cup cooked chopped turkey
3	eggs		
1	tablespoon flour		

Topping (1½ cups cranberry sauce)

1	cup cranberries	2	tablespoons cornstarch
½	cup orange juice	1	tablespoon water
1	tablespoon sugar		

This great dish is perfect for turkey day leftover. The recipe was contributed by Pamela Johnson, chef/owner of Small Planet Deli.

Press stuffing in bottom and halfway up sides of 8-inch spring form pan. Set aside. For filling, sauté onion in butter until soft. In blender or food processor, blend Ricotta cheese, eggs, flour, and salt and pepper until smooth. In a bowl, mix cheese mixture with onion, chives, and turkey. Spoon into prepared crust. Bake at 350° for 50 minutes or until set. Cool. For topping, combine cranberries, orange juice, and sugar in small saucepan. Bring to a boil and simmer 5 minutes. Dissolve cornstarch in water and stir in cranberries. Simmer until thick. Spread on cheesecake and cool.

Can also use chicken.

Yield: 10 to 12 servings

Cranberry Cream Cheese Coffee Cake

Cake

½	cup butter, softened	2	teaspoons baking soda
1	cup sugar	½	teaspoon salt
2	eggs	1	cup milk
2	teaspoons vanilla	1	(12-ounce) package fresh
3	cups flour		cranberries

Filling

8	ounces cream cheese, softened	1	egg
		1	teaspoon vanilla
⅓	cup sugar		

Topping

¼	cup butter, softened	½	cup flour
1	cup sugar	2	teaspoons cinnamon

For batter, cream together butter and sugar. Add eggs and vanilla; mix until light and fluffy. Mix together dry ingredients and slowly beat into batter alternating with milk. Fold in cranberries. For filling, in a medium bowl, beat first 3 filling ingredients until smooth. Add vanilla. For topping, mix all ingredients in a bowl until crumbly. Place ¾ of batter in a greased 9x13 baking dish. Top with cream cheese filling and dot with remaining batter. Sprinkle topping over coffee cake. Bake uncovered at 375° for 1 hour.

Yield: 10 to 12 servings

Bread

Los Barcos-The Christopher Columbus Replicas

More than five hundred years after Christopher Columbus discovered the New World in 1492, we have the opportunity to imagine what his voyage must have been like. Los Carabelas, the Niña, Pinta and Santa Maria, are three full-scale, wooden replicas of the Columbus fleet, and they are here to explore. Each was authentically reproduced by the Spanish government and have been on display since 1993 in Corpus Christi, where they create a sharp contrast to the modern tankers that sail into the port. Walk aboard the Pinta or Santa Maria at The Corpus Christi Museum of Science and History or actually sail the bay on the Niña and take a trip half a century back in time. Each ship is slightly different, for instance, the Santa Maria, Columbus' flagship, is much larger than the other two at ninety-seven feet long. The Niña and the Pinta are seventy and a half feet long and seventy-four and a half feet in length, respectively. However, all three are built of oak and pine planks, hand forged nails and hemp rigging. Their square sails, rope ladders, royal flags and navigational aids are true to the 15th Century construction and technology. Visitors may watch as the two replicas in dry dock are repaired according to the standards of the original explorer's day. It is easy to marvel at how the crews, there were twenty-eight on the Santa Maria and seventeen each on the Niña and Pinta, managed life in such cramped quarters. The men slept on bare decks. On the half-deck of the Santa Maria is the only furniture allowed: a cooking stove, pine table and chairs. More importantly are the navigational instruments of the period that are still used to sail the replicas, including a tide marker, cross staff, astrolabe, quadrant, hourglass, compass, and a zondaleza for measuring speed. Amazingly it was sophisticated enough to land Columbus and his crew on the place that became the New World.

Jalapeño Cheese Bread

½	cup warm water	3½	cups flour, divided
1	package dry yeast	1	teaspoon salt
1	tablespoon sugar	1	cup grated sharp
¼	cup butter		Cheddar cheese
½	cup milk	1	(4-ounce) can jalapeños,
1	egg		drained and chopped

Proof yeast in warm water with sugar. Melt butter with milk and set aside. In bowl or food processor, combine 3 cups of flour, salt, and butter mixture. Gently mix in egg and yeast mixture. Add cheese and jalapeños; knead/process until elastic. Place dough in a greased bowl, turn to coat, cover, and let rise in warm place for 30 minutes. Punch down and place into loaf pans. Cover and allow to rise for 45 minutes or until doubled in bulk. Bake at 350° for 40 minutes.

Yield: 1 large or 2 small loaves

Half the jalapeños makes a flavorful, less spicy bread. Adjust to your preference.

Sweet Potato Bread

1	(15-ounce) can sweet	1	cup milk
	potatoes in heavy syrup	½	cup sugar
2	packages dry yeast	2	teaspoons salt
½	cup warm water	1	teaspoon cinnamon
½	cup butter, melted	6½	cups flour
2	eggs		

Dissolve yeast in warm water. Mash potatoes with their liquid. Add butter and next 3 ingredients to potatoes and blend well. Slowly add yeast mixture. Mix in salt, cinnamon, and flour 1 cup at a time until a soft dough forms. Place in a greased bowl, turn to coat, cover and let rise in warm place for 1 hour. Punch dough down, divide into loaf pans, cover and let rise for 45 minutes, or until doubled in size. Bake at 350° for 40 minutes or until lightly browned.

Yield: 2 large loaves

Grandma Ruby's Dinner Rolls

1	package yeast	¼	teaspoon salt
1	cup warm water, divided	3	tablespoons oil
2	tablespoons sugar	2	cups flour

Dissolve yeast in ¼ cup warm water. Dissolve sugar in remaining ¾ cup warm water. To the yeast mixture, add salt, and oil. Slowly sift in flour. Add sugar/water mixture. Knead about 5 minutes until smooth and elastic. Cover and let rise until double in size. Flour hands, pinch off pieces of dough, roll in flour, and shape into 10 rolls. Place on an ungreased baking sheet and bake at 400° for 15 to 20 minutes.

Yield: 10 rolls

Easy Beer Bread

3	cups self-rising flour	⅓	cup sugar
1	can beer	½	cup butter, melted

Try adding garlic or other herbs.

In bowl, combine first 3 ingredients and mix well. Pour into buttered loaf pan. Cover and let rise 1 hour. Bake at 350° for 20 minutes. Drizzle melted butter over loaf and bake another 20 to 25 minutes.

Yield: 1 loaf

Pan de Campo

4	cups flour	½	cup butter, softened
1	teaspoon salt	½	cup sour cream
4	teaspoons baking powder	1½	cups buttermilk

A traditional Mexican bread cooked over open coals at South Texas ranch camps.

Mix all ingredients until a moist dough forms. Let stand for 15 minutes. Pat into a large ball and place in a jelly roll pan, spreading dough evenly. Bake at 350° for 30 minutes. Cut into squares.

Yield: 6 servings

Sunshine Rolls with Orange Butter

Rolls

2	packages dry yeast	2	eggs, beaten well
1	cup warm water	4	cups flour
1	teaspoon salt	1	teaspoon orange zest, grated
⅓	cup sugar		
⅓	cup vegetable oil		

Orange Butter

¼	cup frozen orange juice, undiluted	¾	cup butter
		1	box powdered sugar

Dissolve yeast in 1 cup lukewarm water. In a large bowl, combine yeast with salt, sugar, oil, and eggs. Gradually add flour and zest. Knead until elastic. Let rise until more than doubled in size. Pinch off and form into rolls. Place on a baking sheet, cover, and let rise again. Bake at 375° until lightly browned, about 15 minutes. To make orange butter, cream orange juice, butter, and sugar. Put in container. Spread on warm rolls. Bake at 375° until brown.

Corpus Christi has two higher level educational institutions, Del Mar Junior College and Texas A&M at Corpus Christi, often referred to as the Island University.

Heavenly Holiday Rolls

	cup shortening, melted	2½	teaspoons salt
3	packages dry yeast	2	eggs, lightly beaten
⅓	cup warm water	2	cups water
5¼	cups bread flour	½	cup butter, melted
½	cup sugar		

Preheat oven to 350°. Dissolve yeast in warm water and let sit 20 minutes. Sift together flour, sugar, and salt, set aside. In small bowl combine eggs and water. With hands, alternate adding small amounts of egg mixture and yeast into dry ingredients. Add shortening a little at a time. Cover and refrigerate 1½ to 2 hours. Take ⅓ of dough and roll out on floured surface to ½ inch thickness. Cut with floured biscuit cutter, dip into melted butter, and arrange on pans. Cover and set in warm place for 1 hour or until doubled in size. Bake at 350° to 375° for about 20 minutes or until brown.

Yield: 2½ to 3 dozen rolls

No kneading needed! Can be made a day or two before baking. Cover with plastic wrap and refrigerate. Remove 20 to 30 minutes before baking.

Classic Scones with Variations

Scones

2	cups flour
2	tablespoons sugar
1	tablespoon baking powder
½	teaspoon salt

4	tablespoons cold unsalted butter
⅓	cup heavy cream
1	egg
1	egg yolk

An epicurean delight from Pamela Johnson of the Small Planet Deli.

Variations

Cinnamon Scones, add:
1   teaspoon cinnamon
Currant Scones, add:
2   tablespoons currants
White Chocolate Scones, add:
1   tablespoon white chocolate chips

Apricot Scones, add:
5   dried apricots, chopped
Blueberry Scones, add:
2   tablespoons dried blueberries

Mix dry ingredients. Cut in butter, cream, egg, and egg yolk until blended and ball forms. Add 1 of the variations at this time. On lightly floured surface shape dough into 1½-inch thick circle. Place on a greased baking sheet and bake at 375° for 15 minutes or until lightly browned. Serve warm with jam and cream cheese, cut into 4 to 8 wedges.

Yield: 4 to 8 scones

Herb Butter

½ cup butter, softened
1 tablespoon snipped chives
2 teaspoons minced parsley
2 teaspoons minced nasturtiums

In a small bowl, blend to-gether all ingredients. Spread on your favorite breads.

Buttermilk Biscuits

2	cups flour
3	teaspoons baking powder
2	teaspoons sugar

½	teaspoon cream of tartar
¼	teaspoon salt
½	cup shortening
¾	cup buttermilk

Preheat oven to 450°. Sift flour with next 4 ingredients. Cut in shortening until mixture resembles coarse crumbs. Make well in center. Add buttermilk stirring just until dough clings together. Knead gently on lightly floured surface, 10 to 12 strokes. Pat to ½ inch thickness. Cut with biscuit cutter, dipping cutter in flour between cuts. Place on ungreased baking sheet. Bake at 450° for 10 to 12 minutes or until brown. Serve warm.

Yield: 10 to 12 biscuits

Southern Biscuits

4	cups flour	2	teaspoons salt
2	tablespoons baking powder	⅔	cup shortening
1	tablespoon sugar	1⅓	cups lowfat milk

Preheat oven to 450°. Sift together dry ingredients. Cut in shortening in food processor or mixer until mixture is crumbly. Slowly add milk until dough forms. Roll out on a lightly floured surface to ¼-inch thickness. Cut with small biscuit cutter. Place on ungreased cookie sheet 1 inch apart and bake 10 to 12 minutes or until brown.

Yield: 3 dozen biscuits

For parties, roll thin, spread top of dough with butter, fold dough in half, and continue according to directions. This method makes a flaky biscuit that opens easily.
Best biscuits south of the Red River!

Jalapeño Cornbread

1	pound ground meat	2	cups grated Cheddar cheese
2	(6-ounce) packages cornbread mix	½	cup chopped onion
2	eggs, beaten	¾	jalapeño, seeded and chopped
⅓	cup sweet milk		
1	(10-ounce) can cream style corn		

Brown meat, drain grease, and set aside. Combine cornbread mix with eggs and milk. Add corn and mix well. Pour half of mixture into greased 9x13 pan. Top with meat, cheese, onions, and jalapeños. Pour in rest of batter and cook at 400° for 20 to 25 minutes.

Splendid addition to a pot luck dinner.

Yield: 12 to 14 servings

Corn Sticks

⅓	cup oil	1	teaspoon baking powder
1	egg	1½	teaspoons baking soda
1¼	cups lowfat milk	½	teaspoon salt
1	cup cornmeal	½	teaspoon sugar
1	cup flour		

Preheat oven to 475°. Lightly grease cast iron corn stick pans. Beat oil and egg together until foamy. Add milk. Sift in dry ingredients and beat until smooth. Heat pans in oven until very hot. Add 2 tablespoons batter to each mold. Bake 6 to 8 minutes. Serve at once with butter and honey or cane syrup.

Yield: 18 servings

Cornmeal pancakes! Leftover batter may be thinned with milk for pancakes.

Husky Cornbread

2	eggs	1	cup cornmeal
1	(8-ounce) carton sour cream	3½	teaspoons baking powder
½	cup corn oil	1	teaspoon salt
1	cup cream style corn		

Combine first 4 ingredients. Add cornmeal, baking powder, and salt. Pour into a 9-inch greased skillet. Bake at 350° for 35 to 40 minutes.

Yield: 6 to 8 servings

Butterscotch Banana Bread

3½ cups all-purpose flour	2 cups mashed ripe bananas
4 teaspoons baking powder	2 eggs
1 teaspoon baking soda	½ cup butter, melted
1 teaspoon cinnamon	½ cup milk
1 teaspoon nutmeg	2⅔ cups chopped pecans, divided
1 teaspoon salt	1 (12-ounce) package butterscotch morsels
1½ cups sugar	

Chocolate chips can be substituted for butter-scotch morsels.

Preheat oven to 350°. Sift together first 6 ingredients and set aside. In separate bowl, combine next 4 ingredients and beat until creamy. Slowly add dry mixture and milk, alternating. Blend well. Stir in 2 cups pecans and butterscotch morsels. Pour batter into 2 greased and floured 9x5 loaf pans. Sprinkle with remaining pecans. Bake 60 to 70 minutes. Cool 10 to 15 minutes before removing from pans.

Yield: 2 loaves

The Great Pumpkin Bread

1 cup vegetable oil	1 teaspoon baking powder
3 cups sugar	1 teaspoon ground cinnamon
4 eggs, beaten	
1 (16-ounce) can pumpkin	1 teaspoon ground cloves
⅔ cup lowfat milk	1 teaspoon ground nutmeg
1 teaspoon vanilla	2 teaspoons salt
3½ cups flour	½ cup pecans, chopped
2 teaspoons baking soda	1 cup raisins (optional)

Will freeze. Serve with butter or softened cream cheese.

Preheat oven to 325°. Grease and lightly flour 2 metal loaf pans. Set aside. Cream oil and sugar. Add eggs, pumpkin, milk, and vanilla and mix well. Sift together dry ingredients and gradually add to pumpkin mix. Stir in nuts and raisins. Pour batter into loaf pans and bake for 1 hour. For tiny loaves, reduce cooking time to 30 to 35 minutes.

Yield: 2 loaves

Cranberry Coconut Bread

1½	cups flour	¼	cup walnut oil
½	cup sugar	1	cup ripe mashed bananas
2	teaspoons baking powder	½	cup dried cranberries
½	teaspoon baking soda	½	cup shredded coconut, lightly toasted
½	teaspoon salt	½	cup chopped walnuts
2	eggs		

In 1899, Captain Richard King of the King Ranch brought the first locomotive for the Texas Mexican Railroad and named it The Corpus Christi.

Preheat oven to 350°. Grease and flour 1 loaf pan. In a large bowl, sift together dry ingredients. In a separate bowl, lightly beat eggs and add remaining ingredients. Combine with dry ingredients. Stir just until flour is moistened. Pour into pan. Bake 50 to 55 minutes. Cool on rack for 10 minutes.

Yield: 1 loaf

Muy Bueno Blueberry Muffins

1	cup sugar	3	eggs
3	cups flour	1	cup milk
2	teaspoons baking powder	⅔	cup oil
1	teaspoon salt	1	(16-ounce) can blueberries, drained

Fresh blueberries may be used instead of canned.

Place dry ingredients in a bowl and mix well. In separate bowl, combine egg, milk, and oil. Add to dry ingredients and stir quickly until moist. Fold in blueberries. Place greased muffin tins in oven for a few minutes to heat. Fill muffin tins ¾ full. Bake at 275° for 25 minutes or until brown.

Yield: 2 dozen muffins

Sugar Top Muffins

1 cup flour	¾ cup milk
1 cup quick oats	⅓ cup vegetable oil
¼ cup brown sugar	½ cup nuts
¼ teaspoon baking powder	1 teaspoon cinnamon
¼ teaspoon baking soda	1 cup sugar
1 egg, beaten	

Grease muffin tin and set aside. In a large bowl, combine first 5 ingredients. In separate bowl, combine egg, milk, and oil. Add to dry ingredients and stir until moistened. Add nuts. Fill muffin cups ⅔ full. Combine cinnamon and 1 cup sugar. Sprinkle tops with the cinnamon/sugar mixture. Bake at 375° for 18 to 20 minutes.

Yield: 16 to 18 muffins

Batter can be stored in refrigerator for 1 week.

Morning Glory Muffins

1 cup flour	2 eggs
½ cup whole wheat flour	¼ cup butter, melted
1 cup sugar	⅓ cup milk
1 teaspoon baking powder	1 cup grated carrots
1 teaspoon baking soda	⅔ cup pineapple, with juice
1 teaspoon cinnamon	1 teaspoon vanilla
½ teaspoon salt	

Mix first 7 ingredients. In separate bowl, combine eggs and remaining ingredients. Pour over dry mixture and stir just until dry ingredients are moistened. Pour into large paper lined muffin tins and bake at 350° for 25 minutes.

Yield: 16 to 18 muffins

Savory Thyme Butter

½ cup butter, softened
1 tablespoon snipped savory
1 teaspoon snipped thyme
1 small clove garlic, minced

In a small bowl, blend together all ingredients. Use on vegetables, warm breads, potatoes, and fish.

French Breakfast Puffs

½	cup vegetable oil		¼	teaspoon nutmeg
1	cup sugar, divided		½	cup milk
1	egg		6	tablespoons butter, melted
1½	cups flour			
1	teaspoon baking powder		1	teaspoon cinnamon
¼	teaspoon salt			

In a large bowl, combine oil, ½ cup sugar, and egg. In separate bowl, sift together next 4 ingredients. Gradually add to egg mixture alternating with milk. Fill greased muffins cups ¾ full. Bake at 350° for 20 to 25 minutes. Mix together the remaining ½ cup sugar and cinnamon. Dip tops of warm muffins in butter then into cinnamon sugar mixture.

Also marvelous as mini muffins.

Yield: 1 dozen puffs

Flour Tortillas

½ teaspoon salt
½-¾ cup warm water
2 cups flour
½ teaspoon baking powder
2 tablespoons shortening

Dissolve salt in warm water. Mix flour and baking powder together. Cut shortening into flour mixture. Slowly add enough water for dough to form a ball. Knead for 1 minute until smooth. Pinch off pieces and roll out on lightly floured surface. Cook on an ungreased skillet until light browned.

Plum Muffins

2	cups sugar		2	small jars baby food plums
2	cups self-rising flour			
1	cup oil		2	teaspoons allspice
3	eggs		1	cup finely chopped walnuts

Combine all ingredients in order listed. Stir well. Fill greased muffin tins half full. Bake 325° for 15 minutes.

Yield: 16 to 18 muffins

Julietta's Cream Cheese Braids

Bread

1	cup sour cream	2	packages dry yeast
½	cup sugar	½	cup lukewarm water
1	teaspoon salt	2	eggs
½	cup butter	4	cups flour

Cream Cheese Filling

2	(8-ounce) packages	1	egg, beaten
	cream cheese, softened	⅛	teaspoon salt
¾	cup sugar	2	teaspoons vanilla

Glaze

2	cups powdered sugar	2	teaspoons vanilla
4	tablespoons milk		

In saucepan, warm sour cream over medium heat. Stir in sugar, salt, and butter. Cool. Sprinkle yeast over warm water. In large bowl, combine yeast with sour cream mixture, eggs, and flour. Mix well. Cover tightly and refrigerate overnight. Divide dough into 4 parts. Roll dough out into rectangles on lightly floured surface. Combine all filling ingredients, mixing well. Spread cream cheese filling in center of each rectangle. Fold over sides and pinch edges to seal. Place seam side down on a baking sheet. Make slits along sides every 2-inches, leaving center intact. Cover and let rise, 1 hour. Bake at 375° for 15 minutes. Combine all glaze ingredients and pour over warm braids.

Yield: 4 braids

Muenster Bread

Bread

2	packages dry yeast	1½	tablespoons sugar
¼	cup warm water	1½	teaspoons salt
1	cup warm milk	½	cup butter, melted
		3½	cups flour

Filling

2	pounds Muenster cheese, grated	1	egg, beaten
		3	tablespoons butter, melted

Dissolve yeast in warm water, set aside. Combine milk and next 3 ingredients in a large bowl. Stir in yeast and add flour, 1 cup at a time, until you have a workable dough. Turn dough out on lightly floured surface and knead until smooth and elastic, about 8 minutes. Place in a greased bowl, turn to coat and let rise in warm place until doubled in size, about 1½ hours. Punch down and let rise 30 minutes more. For filling, combine cheese, egg and butter. Punch dough down again and let rest 15 minutes. On lightly floured surface, roll into 24 to 26-inch circle. Fold dough in half and lay on pizza pan. Unfold and carefully push dough onto outer edges of pan. Mound filling in middle of dough and bring up edges of dough, pleating dough around cheese. Gather dough at top and twist into knob. If dough tears, pinch together. Let rest 15 minutes. Bake at 375° for 1 hour. Cool on rack about 40 minutes.

Do not cut until cheese is cooled.

Yield: 10 to 12 servings

Salads

Farming

Early in its settlement in the mid 1800's, the Coastal Bend was billed as a place for fishing and fun—a cloud nine located by the sea. The settlers who came would soon find clouds of a different sort, the small white tufts of fibrous cotton growing in the South Texas dirt. As valuable as tourism to residents of the entire region, farming became big business by the turn of the century. With the establishments of huge farms and ranches, cotton was the primary money making crop for decades, grown along with smaller vegetable plots and feed grain for local livestock consumption. Livestock, especially cattle, were themselves a valuable commodity. South of Corpus Christi lies one of Texas' as well as the world's largest ranches, King Ranch. It is one of the state's biggest cotton producers and a place where raising cattle is second to few. The Port of Corpus Christi has become a center for agricultural exports, continuing the legacy of those early farms and ranches. The cattle still graze and vast expanses of fertile acres are planted each spring by farmers. They are harvested each summer for hundreds of millions of dollars in receipts. Also very prevalent, is the small scale gardener. In their own backyards, jalapeños, tomatoes, beans, and other vegetables can grow almost year-round. Along the roads, in small towns, and even around larger cities, perfect row after perfect row of tall green stalks or fields of dark, tilled soil stretch to the horizon. South Texas agriculture has changed though. Since the 1930's, sorghum has become the major cash crop for many. It is a sturdy plant that farmers can count on when the weather or other variables threaten alternative crops such as corn or cotton. Of course, technology has made it easier and sometimes necessary for farmers to work larger tracts of land. As a result, the size of the average farm has increased over the years and the number of small farmers has decreased. Working the land is still a family tradition for many South Texans, working sunup to sundown, side by side for the yield of bounty the rich soil allows.

Pear and Chèvre Salad

Salad

6	cups baby greens	½	cup chopped green onion
1	large firm green pear, diced	2	ounces goat cheese
		⅓	cup toasted walnuts

Dressing

½	cup fresh strawberries, stemmed	1	tablespoon sugar
¼	cup white wine vinegar	½	teaspoon salt
½	cup oil	½	teaspoon pepper

Toss greens with pears and onions. Drop goat cheese by the ½ teaspoon into salad. Place all dressing ingredients in blender and pulse until smooth. Shake well before serving. Toss salad with dressing and sprinkle on walnuts.

As the salad is tossed the goat cheese spreads onto the leaves with the dressing.

Yield: 3 to 4 servings

Vegetable gardens are plentiful year round in South Texas. The sub-tropical climate provides for fresh vegetables and citrus all year long.

Lamar Park Salad

3	ears corn, cooked and cut from cob	12	sundried tomatoes, rehydrated
1	bunch arugula	3	tablespoons balsamic vinegar
1	bunch red leaf lettuce		
2	bunches watercress	8	large fresh basil leaves
½	cup red wine vinegar	⅓	cup olive oil
1	large shallot		

Combine corn and next 3 ingredients in large bowl. Place all remaining ingredients in a blender or food processor and pulse. Toss salad with dressing.

Yield: 4 to 6 servings

Something light to titillate your taste buds!

Mykonos Salad

Salad

½	head iceberg lettuce, washed and torn
½	head romaine lettuce, washed and torn
2-3	tomatoes, quartered
1	medium onion, sliced thin

1	bell pepper, sliced thin
1	cucumber, sliced thin
1	cup Calamata olives
3	tablespoons capers
4	ounces Feta cheese

Calamata olives are large dark green olives. Guest need to be warned of the pit.

Dressing

½	cup olive oil

¼	cup salad vinegar
	salt and pepper to taste

Toss lettuces with next 6 ingredients. Combine all dressing ingredients and pour over salad. Crumble Feta cheese over top and garnish with extra olives.

Yield: 6 servings

Strawberry Almond Salad

Dressing

¾	cup oil
6	tablespoon sugar
6	tablespoons vinegar

1½	teaspoons salt
	pepper to taste
	dash of Tabasco

Salad

1½	cups sliced almonds
9	tablespoons sugar
1	head Bibb lettuce, torn
1	head red leaf lettuce, torn
1	head green leaf lettuce, torn

2	cups chopped celery
6	green onions, chopped
1	pint strawberries, quartered

Combine all dressing ingredients and chill. In a small pan, over medium heat, toast almonds with sugar, stirring constantly until sugar dissolves. Cool and crumble almonds. Toss remaining salad ingredients just before serving. Add almond and toss with dressing.

Spinach can be used in place of one lettuce.

Yield: 10 to 12 servings

Red Heart Salad

Salad

1-2	heads red leaf lettuce	1	red onion, sliced
1	(14½-ounce) can hearts of palm, drained and sliced lengthwise	1	red bell pepper, seeded and diced
18	thin fresh asparagus spears	6	green onions, sliced with tops

Dressing

5	tablespoons olive oil	¼	teaspoon white pepper
3	tablespoons wine vinegar	½	teaspoon Spike seasoning
2	tablespoons fresh lime juice	½	teaspoon oregano
5	cloves garlic	½	teaspoon dried mustard
¼	teaspoon salt		

Place 1 large lettuce leaf on each plate and tear other leaves into 1-inch pieces and lay on top of single leaf. Lay 1-2 slices heart of palm and 3 asparagus spears over lettuce. Top with onion rings, red pepper, and green onions. Combine all dressing ingredients in blender and mix well. Top salad with dressing.

Garnish with tomato wedge, green or black olives, or egg slices.

Yield: 6 servings

Turn this attractive salad into a main course by adding strips of cooked chicken or ham.

Italian Spinach Salad

1	large head leaf lettuce, torn	1	(4-ounce) can sliced black olives, drained
2	pound spinach, torn (14-ounce) can artichokes, drained and quartered	½	pound mushrooms, sliced
		1	bottle of your favorite Italian dressing

Place lettuce and spinach in separate bags and refrigerate overnight. Pour dressing over artichokes, olives, and mushrooms, cover, and refrigerate up to 24 hours. Toss greens with salad 5 minutes before serving.

Yield: 8 servings

Sesame Slaw

Salad

3	cups shredded cabbage mix	1	medium red bell pepper, julienned
¼	pound snow peas, trimmed and cut in julienne strips	4	green onions, chopped
		2	tablespoons sesame seeds, toasted

Add 1½ cups slivered pork or chicken for a main course salad.

Dressing

¼	cup chicken broth	1	tablespoon peanut oil
¼	cup rice wine vinegar	1	tablespoon sesame oil
3	tablespoons soy sauce		

Combine salad ingredients in a large bowl. Combine all dressing ingredients in jar. Cover and shake well before pouring over salad.

Yield: 6 servings

Sunflower Spinach Salad

Salad

½	pound mushrooms, sliced	½	pound bacon, fried crisp and crumbled
3	tablespoons lemon juice	1	medium red onion, chopped
1	pound spinach, washed and torn	3	tablespoons sunflower seeds, toasted
1	head iceberg lettuce, washed and torn		

Dressing

½	cup red wine vinegar	1	teaspoon dry mustard
1	tablespoons celery seed	1	small red onion, sliced
½	cup sugar	1	cup oil
1	teaspoon salt		

Sauté mushrooms in lemon juice until soft. Combine mushrooms and remaining salad ingredients in large bowl. Set aside. Boil vinegar with celery seed until reduced by half. Remove from heat and cool. Place sugar and next 3 ingredients in blender. Slowly add vinegar and purée With motor running, add oil. Blend on high 1 minute. Refrigerate. Pour dressing over salad just before serving.

Garnish with a dollop of sour cream.

Yield: 8 servings

Feta Chicken and Asparagus Salad

1½	pounds boneless, skinless chicken breast	2	heads Boston lettuce, torn
1	teaspoon salt	1	cup sliced Roma tomatoes
1	teaspoon pepper	½	cup chopped red onion
¼	cup olive oil	½	cup crumbled Feta cheese
3	tablespoons lemon juice	2	teaspoons finely chopped fresh rosemary
½	pound asparagus, cut in 1-inch pieces		

Season chicken breasts with salt and pepper. Marinate chicken in oil and lemon juice for 1 hour. Grill over hot coals until done, but not dry. Slice breasts diagonally and set aside. Place asparagus in boiling water for 2 minutes, then rinse under cold water. Set aside. Divide lettuce among salad plates and top with next 4 ingredients. Top with grilled chicken slices and asparagus. Drizzle with Honey Mustard Vinaigrette before serving.

Yield: 4 to 6 main course servings

Honey Mustard Vinaigrette

⅓	cup red wine vinegar	½	cup olive oil
1	tablespoon honey	1	teaspoon lemon pepper
1	tablespoon Dijon mustard	1	teaspoon salt

Combine all ingredients in a small bowl. Chill. Whisk before serving.

Yield: 1 cup

Try this delightful dressing on your favorite green salad.

Picnic Pasta Salad

4-6 chicken breasts
1 pound vermicelli, broken in thirds and cooked
½ cup chopped bell pepper
2 cups chopped celery
6-8 green onions, chopped
3 hard boiled eggs
1 (2-ounce) jar pimentos, drained
¾ cup slivered almonds, toasted
1 quart ranch style dressing

This is a perfect luncheon salad.

Boil chicken for 30 minutes. Cool, bone, and cut in bite-size pieces. Combine all salad ingredients and toss well with dressing.

Boiled shrimp can be substituted for chicken.

Yield: 15 to 20 servings

Mandarin Chicken Salad

Salad
1½ pounds skinless, boneless chicken breasts
1 (14-ounce) can chicken broth
½ cups walnuts, toasted
1 head red leaf lettuce, torn
1 (8-ounce) can Mandarin oranges, drained
2 stalks celery, chopped
2 scallions, chopped

Dressing
1¼ cups low fat, plain yogurt
1 tablespoon honey
salt and pepper

Poach chicken in broth for 30 minutes. Drain and slice in 1-inch strips. Combine lettuce with next 3 ingredients. In small bowl, mix yogurt, honey, salt and pepper. Pour dressing over chicken. Toss chicken with lettuce mixture. Top with walnuts and serve.

Yield: 4 servings

Hoisin Shredded Chicken Salad

Salad

2	whole, boneless, skinless chicken breasts	½	cup chopped green onions
¼	cup soy sauce	¼	bunch cilantro, chopped
1	clove garlic, crushed	1	tablespoon toasted sesame seeds
4	teaspoons sugar		
1	tablespoon sherry	¼	cup slivered almonds, toasted
1	teaspoon Hoisin sauce		
1	small head iceberg lettuce, torn	2½	cups Mai Foo (rice sticks) -or- crispy Chinese noodles

Dressing

2	teaspoons Chinese hot mustard	1	tablespoon sesame oil
1	teaspoon Hoisin sauce	2	tablespoons red wine vinegar
½	teaspoon salt	1	tablespoon vegetable oil
½	teaspoon sugar		

Mix soy sauce, garlic, sugar, sherry and Hoisin sauce and pour over chicken breasts. Bake at 350° for 35 minutes. Let cool and shred chicken. Pour small amount of pan juices over chicken to keep moist. Fry rice sticks and store in airtight container or use crispy Chinese noodles. Mix dressing ingredients together and pour over chicken. Combine chicken with salad greens, onion, cilantro, nuts and sesame seeds and toss well. Top with crisp rice sticks or crispy Chinese noodles.

Yield: 6 servings

Addictive Almond Chicken Salad

	cups diced, cooked chicken	4	tablespoons chopped fresh parsley
	cups chopped celery	4	tablespoons lemon juice
	cup slivered almonds	¼	teaspoon salt
⅓	cups mayonnaise	1	teaspoon white pepper

In large mixing bowl, toss chicken, celery, and almonds. Combine mayonnaise, parsley, lemon juice, salt and pepper. Combine mayonnaise mixture with chicken and toss well. Refrigerate 1 hour.

Best if made the day before serving.

Yield: 8 servings

Shrimp Salad with Avocado Vinaigrette

Salad

2	pounds medium shrimp, boiled, peeled, and cut in half	1	head green leaf lettuce, torn
1	head Boston lettuce, torn	2	cups tomatoes, cubed
		2	cups croutons

Arrange shrimp with lettuce and tomato wedges in salad bowl/plate and toss with Avocado Vinaigrette. Sprinkle on croutons.

Vinaigrette

1	large avocado, peeled and seeded	3	cloves garlic
¼	cup fresh lime juice	¾	cup olive oil
¼	cup white wine vinegar		pinch of salt
1	tablespoon freash basil		pinch of pepper

Place all dressing ingredients in blender, except oil, and blend until smooth. With motor running, slowly add oil.

Yield: 4 salad servings

Homemade croutons are superior to anything that can be bought at the store. Try the Parmesan Dill Croutons on page 82.

¡VIVA! Tradiciones

Shrimp Salad Vermicelli

Salad

2	pounds shrimp, boiled, peeled, and cut in half	⅓	cup chopped red bell pepper
12	ounces vermicelli, broken, cooked and drained	½	cup chopped green onion
1	cup chopped celery	¼	cup capers, drained
		2	hard boiled eggs, chopped
			tomato slices for garnish

Dressing

¾	cup mayonnaise	2	teaspoons seasoned salt
2	tablespoons lime juice	1	teaspoon cracked black pepper
1	clove garlic, minced		
⅓	cup oil		

Mix dressing ingredients and refrigerate. Combine all salad ingredients in a large bowl and toss with dressing. Arrange tomato slices over salad.

Yield: 8 servings

Shrimp Desirée

4	pounds shrimp, cooked and peeled	1	(3-ounce) jar capers, drained
½	cup chopped celery	1½	cups oil
1	cup chopped onion	½	cup salad vinegar
½	cup pimento-stuffed olives, cut in half	½	teaspoon Tabasco
1	red bell pepper, cubed	2	teaspoons lemon juice
1	bell pepper, cubed	¼	cup lime juice
		1	tablespoon garlic powder
		1	tablespoon celery seed

Combine ingredients in order listed, toss well. Cover and refrigerate 24 hours. To serve, arrange lettuce leaves on platter and top with marinated shrimp mixture.

Be sure to have lots of crusty bread to serve with this salad.

Yield: 8 servings

Serve this salad over rice or greens for a complete meal. An excellent change for a ladies luncheon.

Crab Toss

3	tablespoons sour cream	1	cup cooked rice
¾	cup mayonnaise	1	(10-ounce) package
1	tablespoon Nature's		frozen peas, thawed
	Seasoning	3	stalks celery, chopped
1	tablespoon lemon juice	¼	cup chopped green onion
1	cup fresh lump crab meat	lettuce leaves	

Combine sour cream, mayonnaise, seasoning, and lemon juice. Toss with remaining ingredients, except lettuce, and refrigerate 24 hours. Serve on lettuce leaves.

Yield: 4 servings

Fluffly Fruit Salad

2½	cups small	1	pint whipping cream
	marshmallows	5-6	bananas, sliced
1	large can crushed	1	cup chopped pecans
	pineapple		

Kids' favorite way to eat fruit.

In large bowl, pour pineapple with juice over marshmallows. Cover with plastic wrap and refrigerate overnight. When almost ready to serve, whip cream until stiff peaks form and fold into pineapple mixture. Add bananas and pecans, mixing gently.

For color, add ½ cup maraschino cherries.

Yield: 6 to 8 servings

Avocado Almond Salad

1	head lettuce, torn	⅓	cup sliced almonds
1	avocado, diced	1	red onion, sliced thin
¼	cup raisins, (optional)	½	cup poppy seed dressing
1	(8-ounce) can Mandarin		
	oranges		

Combine first 6 ingredients and toss lightly with poppy seed dressing.

May garnish with tomato wedges.

Yield: 4 servings

Cucumber Crunch Salad

1	cup mayonnaise	1	small red onion, sliced
¾	cup apple cider vinegar	1	tablespoon coarse black
2	large cucumbers, peeled		pepper
	and sliced	1	head red leaf lettuce

Mix mayonnaise and vinegar until smooth. Add cucumbers, onions, and pepper; blend well. Chill 30 minutes. Place cucumber mixture on bed of lettuce.

Reduce moisture from cucumbers by draining on paper towels after slicing.

Yield: 8 to 12 servings

When your summer garden has been taken over by cucumber plants, double this salad and invite your friends over for lunch.

Antipasto Salad

	bell pepper, chopped	1	small zucchini, sliced
	small onion, chopped	2	Roma tomatoes,
	(4-ounce) can black		quartered
	olives, drained	¼	cup Italian dressing
	(6-ounce) jar artichoke	4	cups salad greens
	hearts, drained		

Toss vegetables with dressing and refrigerate. Serve over mixed greens.

Yield: 4 to 6 servings

Carry Berry Salad

½	pounds carrots, sliced	½	cup minced, fresh
	thin		parsley
⅓	cup olive oil	⅓	cup minced green onions
	tablespoons raspberry		salt and pepper to taste
	vinegar		

Boil carrots until crisp tender. Drain. While still hot, toss carrots with oil and vinegar. Cool. Add parsley, green onion, salt and pepper. Toss gently and refrigerate. Serve at room temperature or cold.

Can be made up to 4 days in advance

Yield: 4 to 6 servings

A carrot lover's salad.

Salad Niçoise

Salad

3-4	boiled new potatoes, sliced	8	ounces black or Greek olives
1	head leaf lettuce	3	hard boiled eggs, sliced
1	large cucumber, peeled and slice	16	ounces albacore tuna, drained
3	tomatoes, sliced	1	small red onion, sliced
¾	pound green beans, blanched	3	tablespoons capers
			fresh basil sprigs

Dressing

¼	cup wine vinegar	¼	teaspoon salt
¾	cup virgin olive oil	⅛	teaspoon pepper

Mix all dressing ingredients and chill a few hours before serving. Marinate potatoes in half of dressing. Cover a platter or tray with lettuce leaves. Arrange vegetables and eggs over lettuce. Place tuna in center. Garnish with onion rings, capers, and basil. Drizzle with remaining dressing.

For a Greek twist, add 8 ounces Feta cheese to dressing.

Yield: 8 to 10 servings

This is a beautiful main dish salad from Nice, France. Great served at a luncheon or on a summer evening.

Black-eyed Pea Salad

10	ounces fresh or frozen black-eyed peas, cooked	½	teaspoon basil
4	medium Roma tomatoes	1	teaspoon parsley
½	cup chopped sweet onion	½	cup olive oil
½	cup chopped celery	⅓	cup red wine vinegar
3	cloves garlic, minced		salt and pepper to taste
½	teaspoon oregano	1	head red leaf lettuce

Black-eyed peas are a southern tradition, always found on the table on New Years Day.

Place drained peas and tomatoes in a large bowl, Add remaining ingredients, except lettuce, and toss gently. Refrigerate at least 4 hours. Serve on a bed of lettuce.

Yield: 6 servings

Broccoli and Grape Salad

½	cup mayonnaise	½	cup celery
1	tablespoon vinegar	½	cup chopped green onions
2	tablespoons sugar		
1	bunch fresh broccoli, chopped and blanched	8	ounces bacon, fried crisp and crumbled (optional)
1½	cups seedless grapes, halved	¼	cup slivered almonds

Combine mayonnaise, vinegar, and sugar in bowl. Toss with broccoli, grapes, celery, and onion. Fold in bacon and almonds before serving.

Yield: 4 to 6 servings

An amazing combination of broccoli and fruit that will surprise even the most fervent broccoli hater.

Orzo Extravaganza

Salad

1	cup orzo, cooked	1	(6-ounce) can tuna, drained
½	pound green beans, cut in 1-inch pieces	1	red bell pepper, chopped
1	(6-ounce) jar marinated artichoke hearts, drained and chopped	⅓	cup black olives

Dressing

2	tablespoons red wine vinegar	1	tablespoon Dijon mustard
1	tablespoon fresh lemon juice	1	clove garlic, minced
4	anchovy filets, chopped	¼	cup olive oil

Place orzo, green beans, and remaining salad ingredients in a large bowl. Set aside. Place vinegar and next 4 ingredients in blender, pulse. With motor running, add oil and blend until emulsified. Pour dressing over orzo mixture and toss well.

Garnish with chopped tomatoes.

Yield: 4 to 6 servings

A great twist on a Niçoise salad. Orzo is tiny rice-shaped pasta.

Summer Pasta Salad

Salad

2	cup fresh snow peas	1	(8-ounce) package cheese stuffed tortellini, cooked
2	cups broccoli florets		
2½	cups cherry tomatoes, halved	3	ounces fettucine, broken and cooked
2	cups fresh mushrooms, quartered	1	tablespoon Parmesan cheese
1	(8-ounce) can black olives, drained		

Dressing

½	cup sliced green onions	2	teaspoons dried basil
⅓	cup red wine vinegar	1	teaspoon dried dill weed
⅓	cup vegetable oil	1	teaspoon salt
⅓	cup olive oil	½	teaspoon pepper
2	tablespoons chopped fresh parsley	½	teaspoon sugar
		½	teaspoon dried oregano
2	cloves garlic, minced	½	teaspoon Dijon mustard

For dressing, combine ingredients in a jar and cover tightly. Shake vigorously until well blended. For salad, drop snow peas in boiling water, boil 1 minute, remove and rinse under cold water. Follow same procedure with broccoli. Combine blanched peas and broccoli with remaining salad ingredients. Toss with dressing and serve.

Yield: 12 servings

Heritage Park is an area of historic homes which have been moved and restored. They represent the ethnic and cultural diversity of Corpus Christi and are recorded Texas Historic Landmarks.

Pasta Insalata

2 cups multi-colored bow tie or corkscrew pasta
2 tablespoons olive oil
2 cups Southwest Relish

Cook pasta according to package directions, drain and toss with oil. Before serving toss with Southwest Relish.

Southwest Relish

2	cups whole kernel corn	¼	cup chopped green olives
2	cups black beans, cooked		
		¼	cup chopped black olives
1	cup garbanzo beans, cooked	⅔	cup white wine vinegar
		⅓	cup olive oil
1	cup pico de gallo	1	tablespoon sugar

Mix vinegar, oil and sugar until sugar dissolves. Place all vegetables in a large bowl and pour dressing over. Refrigerate overnight. Serve as a cold side dish to ham, chicken, fish, and Mexican food.

Yield: 6½ cups

Garlic Bow Ties

Salad

¾ pound bow tie pasta, cooked

2 (6-ounce) jars marinated artichoke hearts

1 (7-ounce) can hearts of palm, drained and sliced

1 (6-ounce) can sliced water chestnuts, drained

¾ cup chopped celery

4 heads endive
pink peppercorns, crushed

Dressing

1½ cups mayonnaise

4 cloves garlic, minced

oil from artichokes

This salad is white, so you can create your own look with garnishes such as tomatoes, black olives, and fresh basil leaves.

Combine mayonnaise, garlic, and oil drained from artichokes. Combine pasta with ⅓ dressing. Chill overnight. Combine quartered artichokes, hearts of palm, water chestnuts, and celery with remaining mayonnaise mixture and chill overnight. Remove 20 minutes before serving and gently toss together. Serve on endive leaves and garnish with peppercorns.

Be sure to let sit 24 hours to let the garlic really flavor things up.

Yield: 8 to 10 servings

Tortellini Salad

Salad

8 ounces cheese filled tortellini, cooked

4 ounces rotini pasta, cooked

8 leaves fresh basil, chopped

4 green onions, chopped

½ cup Parmesan cheese, grated

Dressing

⅓ cup red wine vinegar

¼ cup olive oil

1 garlic clove, minced

1 tablespoon Dijon mustard

Combine dressing ingredients in a jar and shake well. Pour over warm pasta. Add basil and onions and toss. Top with cheese and toss again before serving.

Best made ahead to blend flavors.

Yield: 4 to 6 servings

Pastacelli Salad

Salad

12 ounces vermicelli, cooked al dente
1   cup finely chopped bell pepper
2   cups finely chopped celery

1   (8-ounce) can chopped black olives, drained
1   (2-ounce) jar pimentos, drained
1   (6-ounce) can chopped water chestnuts, drained

Dressing

1   cup mayonnaise
4   tablespoons oil

3   tablespoons lemon juice
1   tablespoon Accent

Combine all dressing and toss with cooked pasta. Refrigerate overnight. Add remaining salad ingredients and toss well before serving.

Yield: 8 servings

Rio Grande Potato Salad

The Rio Grande Valley and Mexico provide South Texas with an abundance of fresh vegetables and fruits year round.

Dressing

1   cup mayonnaise
1   cup sour cream
3   tablespoons lime juice

2   cloves garlic, minced
1   tablespoon mustard

Salad

6   cups new potatoes, washed and boiled with skin
1   cup chopped tomato
½   cup chopped green onions

¼   cup chopped cilantro
1   (4-ounce) can chopped green chilies
1   red bell pepper, diced
2   hard boiled eggs, chopped

Mix all dressing ingredients and refrigerate. Cut boiled potatoes in 1-inch cubes. Combine potatoes with remaining ingredients in a large bowl. Toss with dressing and refrigerate.

Garnish with black olives, onion slices, and tomatoes slices.

Yield: 10 to 12 servings

¡VIVA! Tradiciones

Von Blucher Potato Salad

2	cups cooked new potatoes, cubed	2	tablespoons chopped chives
2	tablespoons finely chopped red onion	1	teaspoon olive oil
1½	tablespoons white wine vinegar	¼	teaspoon sugar
		¼	teaspoon salt
		¼	teaspoon pepper

Place potatoes and onion in large bowl and set aside. Combine vinegar with remaining ingredients. Stir well and pour over potatoes. Toss gently to coat all ingredients.

Yield: 4 servings

The Bluchers, a pioneer family of Corpus Christi, donated two historic homes to the Junior League of Corpus Christi which have been restored to their late 1800's period. One of the homes serves as the headquarters for the Junior League, the other as a nature center for bird watchers.

Cilantro Dressing

1	clove garlic	1	bunch cilantro, trimmed
1	slice onion	1	egg
¾	cup oil	1	teaspoon powdered chicken bouillon
1	tablespoon vinegar		

Combine all ingredients in a blender and purée. Pour into a covered container and shake well before serving.

Will keep 1 week in refrigerator.

Yield: 1 cup

Blue Cheese Dressing

1	quart mayonnaise	½	teaspoon salt
5	ounces blue cheese		juice of 1 lemon
1	cup buttermilk		

Blend all ingredients in blender until smooth. Refrigerate. Serve as a salad dressing or as a dip for raw vegetables.

For a chunky dressing, add crumbled blue cheese after blending.

Yield: 1½ quarts

This recipe from the old Privateer's Club surpasses anything offered in restaurants today.

Roquefort Dressing

1	cup evaporated milk		dash of garlic powder
½	cup vegetable oil	½	cup crumbled Roquefort
¼	cup white vinegar		or blue cheese
½	teaspoon salt		

Blend all ingredients in a food processor until smooth. Add ¼ cup more crumbled cheese after blending for more texture.

Yield: 2 cups

Parmesan Peppercorn Dressing

1	cup mayonnaise	2	teaspoons cracked black
¼	cup Parmesan cheese		pepper
1	tablespoon lemon juice	1	clove garlic, minced
		½	teaspoon dried basil

Combine all ingredients and mix well. Refrigerate several hours for flavors to meld.

Yield: 1½ cups

Parmesan Dill Croutons

½	cup butter, softened		fresh chopped dill weed to
1	cup Parmesan cheese		taste
	minced garlic to taste	1	loaf French bread, sliced
			thin

Combine first 4 ingredients until smooth. Spread on bread slices and cut in 1-inch cubes. Place on a cookie sheet and bake at 350° until lightly browned.

Soups and Sandwiches

Backyard Barbeques and Entertaining South Texas Style

What a better place to get the real flavor of South Texas lifestyle than at a barbeque. From food to folly, barbeques hint to the popular choice of down home family fun. Cooking on the grill is a tradition as old as hunting, whether for necessity, sport, or with a barbeque specifically in mind. Years ago, it was the natural ending to a hunting expedition. Today, it is the time to invite the extended family and friends for a gathering that is too big for the kitchen. Selected cuts of beef, pork, barbacoa, chicken, and wild turkey are grilled over an open fire for a period of hours or more quickly in a 55-gallon oil drum cut in half and made into a Texas sized barbeque pit. Another big favorite is cabrito, or baby goat cooked in a pit that is dug out of the ground. It's a South Texas original. As large as these outdoor fiestas can be, the art of the barbeque has not been lost on urbanites living in relatively small places. Even in enclosed backyards or apartment terraces, South Texans like to cook outdoors—be it to enjoy meat with the distinctive mesquite flavor or to enjoy the party atmosphere that is automatically associated with the gathering because of the almost tropical climate, outdoor parties can be scheduled and held impromptu year round. Celebratory tail-gate parties that gather multiple family members to share food, drink and laughs have preceeded the opening parade of the annual Buccaneer Days festival for decades. In the Coastal Bend, the shoreline is a choice setting for all sorts of outdoor parties, such as the Fourth of July picnics and Bayfest. Night-time bonfires include salty but cooling swims, sand volleyball, friendly song, and conversation around the fire.

¡VIVA! Tradiciones

Poblano Pepper Soup

3-4	poblano peppers, seeded and diced	2	tablespoons cilantro, chopped
¼	cup sliced carrot	¾	cup heavy cream
⅓	cup chopped onion		salt and pepper to taste
3	cloves chopped garlic		Toppings: grated Monterey
1	tablespoon olive oil		Jack cheese, chopped
2	tablespoons flour		cooked chicken, sliced
4	cups chicken broth		avocado, chopped
			tomatoes, tortilla strips

Sauté first 4 ingredients in oil for 5 minutes. Add flour and sauté additional 5 minutes. Add chicken broth to pan and simmer 30 minutes. Purée mixture in blender. Add cilantro, cream, salt, and pepper to blender and pulse. Ladle into soup bowls. Serve with any or all of toppings.

Yield: 4 to 6 servings

Poblano peppers are large dark green mild peppers. Larger peppers do not have the heat of smaller peppers, such as chili pequins.

Taco Soup

1½	pounds ground beef	2	cups water
1	(10½-ounce) can kidney beans, undrained	1	(1½-ounce) package taco seasoning
2	(10½-ounce) can ranch style beans, undrained	1	(1-ounce) package ranch dressing
1	(10½-ounce) can hominy, undrained		Toppings: chopped avocado, sour cream, grated
1	(10½-ounce) can tomatoes with green chilies		Monterey Jack cheese or crumbled corn chips

Brown and drain meat. Combine meat and remaining ingredients in a large pot. Simmer 1 hour. Ladle into soup bowls and serve with choice of toppings.

Yield: 12 to 15 servings

Good for a covered dish or feeding a large crowd.

Tortilla Soup

1	medium onion, chopped	1	teaspoon chili powder
1	(4-ounce) can chopped green chilies	1	teaspoon salt
4	cloves garlic, minced	½	teaspoon ground white pepper
2	tablespoons olive oil	2	teaspoons chopped cilantro
2	(14½-ounce) cans diced tomatoes	2	teaspoons Worcestershire sauce
1	(10½-ounce) can beef broth	1	tablespoon steak sauce
2	cups chicken broth	8	tortillas, cut in 1-inch strips, fried
2	cubes chicken bouillon	1	cup grated sharp Cheddar cheese
1	(8-ounce) can tomato juice		
1	teaspoon ground cumin		

Sauté onion, chilies and garlic in oil until transparent. Add tomatoes, broth, bouillon, tomato juice and seasonings. Bring to boil and reduce heat to simmer. Cook covered for 1 hour. Add water for thinning, if desired. Fry tortilla strips and drain. Serve in soup bowls and top with tortillas and cheese.

If fresh cilantro is not available, use 1 teaspoon dried cilantro or parsley.

Yield: 6 to 8 servings

Shredded chicken can be added for a main course soup.

Chicken and Black Bean Soup

2	chicken breasts with ribs	1	ounce smoked bacon, diced
6	cups water	2	(16-ounce) cans black beans, drained
2	large carrots, sliced	1	tablespoon chopped cilantro
4	large tomatoes, peeled and chopped	¼	cup grated Cheddar or crumbled goat cheese
½	onion, chopped		
4	cloves garlic, minced		

Boil chicken in 5 cups water for 20 minutes. Remove chicken and set aside. Reserve broth. Add carrots and next 5 ingredients to 4 cups of reserved broth and simmer 20 minutes. Skin and bone chicken, cut into bite-size pieces. Add chicken and cilantro to soup. Heat through. Ladle into bowls and garnish with cheese.

Can also garnish with red pepper flakes.

Yield: 4 servings

Green Chili Cheese Soup

1½	tablespoons butter	1	(4-ounce) can chopped green chilies
1½	tablespoons olive oil		
1½	medium yellow onions, chopped	2	small white potatoes, cubed
4	cloves garlic, chopped	1	tablespoon chopped cilantro
3½	cups vegetable or chicken broth	¼	teaspoon cumin
1½	pounds tomatoes, chopped	4	ounces Monterey Jack cheese, cubed

Heat butter and oil in a large stock pot. Sauté onion and garlic for several minutes, then add broth. Pulse tomatoes and chilies in a food processor. Add tomato mixture to soup with potato, cumin, and cilantro. Simmer 30 minutes. Divide cheese among 4 soup bowls. Pour hot soup over cheese and serve immediately.

Yield: 4 servings

In colonial America, chilies were grown by Thomas Jefferson, who imported seeds from Mexico and planted them at Monticello in Virginia.

Caldo con Pollo

1	2½ pound whole chicken	2	cups grated cabbage
1	tablespoon salt	1½	cups sliced carrots
1	tablespoon cumin	1	medium onion, sliced
1	cube chicken bouillon	1½	cups diced green bell pepper
½	teaspoon chopped basil		
3	bay leaves	1	(17-ounce) can garbanzo beans, drained
5	cloves garlic, minced		
1	tablespoon oregano	4	cups cooked rice
½	teaspoon ground cloves		chopped cilantro to taste
2	cups sliced zucchini		

Place first 6 ingredients with 10 cups of water in large pot. Combine garlic, oregano, and cloves with small amount of water to make paste. Add to ingredients in pot and bring to boil, reduce heat to medium and cook for 45 minutes. Remove chicken and skin, bone, and chop. Add zucchini and next 6 ingredients to broth. Bring to a boil and simmer an additional 15 minutes. Return chicken to soup and heat thoroughly. Pour soup over rice.

Top with chopped green onions, diced tomatoes, cilantro, chopped and seeded serrano chilies, or diced avocados.

Yield: 10 to 12 servings

A South Texas favorite Mexican soup.

Tomato Coriander Soup

½   cup chopped celery
3   large green onions,
     minced
2-3 cloves garlic, chopped
2   tablespoons chopped
     parsley
2   tablespoons oregano
1   teaspoon dried coriander
2   tablespoons butter

3   large tomatoes, seeded
     and chopped
1   tablespoon tomato paste
4   cups chicken broth
4   tablespoons olive oil
salt and pepper to taste
sour cream
fresh cilantro

Sauté first 6 ingredients in butter. Combine sautéed mixture and remaining ingredients in large pot, cook over medium heat for 45 minutes. Purée soup in small batches. Serve warm with a spoon of sour cream and fresh cilantro.

Yield: 4 servings

At the turn of the century, beach parties were the center of Corpus Christians' social life with cookouts, shrimp boils, gumbo and chowder parties.

Potato Jalapeño Soup

1   large onion, chopped
3   celery stalks, finely
     chopped
½   cup butter or margarine
5   large baking potatoes,
     peeled and cut into
     medium pieces

8   cups chicken broth
1   teaspoon cumin
⅓   cup chopped, pickled
     jalapeño
4   cups evaporated milk
pinch of baking soda
salt and pepper to taste

In large stock pot, sauté onion and celery in butter until soft. Add potatoes, broth, and cumin. Bring to a boil, cover, and simmer 20 to 30 minutes, or until potatoes are tender. Add jalapeños, soda, and evaporated milk. Coarsely mash potatoes. Season with salt and pepper. Simmer 15 minutes, stirring frequently.

Garnish with finely chopped green onions and dash of paprika.

Yield: 16 servings

¡VIVA! Tradiciones

Dove Gumbo

30	doves, cleaned	1	(14-ounce) can diced tomatoes
3	onions, quartered, divided	4	green onions, chopped
4	stalks celery, quartered, divided	½	teaspoon cayenne pepper
2	teaspoons peppercorns	2	tablespoons chopped parsley
1	bay leaf	1	can beer
⅔	cup flour		salt to taste
½	cup oil	2	cups okra, fresh or frozen
2	cloves garlic, minced		hot cooked rice
1	gallon chicken or beef broth		filé powder (optional)

Cover doves with water seasoned with 1 quartered onion, 2 stalks celery with leaves, peppercorns, and 1 bay leaf. Boil until doves are tender, about 1 hour. Remove dove and bone. Strain broth and reserve liquid. Make a roux by sautéing flour in oil until coffee colored, stirring constantly. Add 2 diced onions and remaining celery to roux and cook until onion is transparent. Add chicken broth to reserved liquid to make 1 gallon. Gradually add roux to broth in small batches stirring constantly to avoid lumps. Add dove meat, tomatoes, and all remaining ingredients, except okra. Simmer on stovetop for 3 hours. Add okra in last hour. Serve over hot rice. Sprinkle with filé powder.

Roux is best made in a cast iron skillet.

Yield: 10 servings

Tortellini Soup

1	large onion, coarsely chopped	1	(14½-ounce) can stewed tomatoes
2	garlic cloves, minced	⅓	cup picante sauce
1	tablespoon olive oil	1	teaspoon dried basil
3	(14-ounce) cans beef broth	1	(7-ounce) package cheese-filled tortellini
			Parmesan cheese

Sauté onion and garlic in olive oil until soft. Add broth, tomato, picante, and basil. Bring to a boil. Add tortellini and simmer 20 minutes until tortellini is done. Remove from heat and serve with a sprinkle of Parmesan cheese.

This soup freezes well.

Yield: 4 to 6 servings

Serve with salad and bread.

Soups and Sandwiches

Pasta Fagioli Soup

1	tablespoon olive oil	6	cups hot water
1	garlic clove, minced	3½	tablespoons instant beef
1	pound lean ground beef		bouillon
1	medium onion, chopped	3½	tablespoons dried
3	celery stalks, chopped		oregano
3	carrots, chopped	2	teaspoons black pepper
2	(14½-ounce) cans diced	2	tablespoons chopped
	tomatoes		parsley
2	(14½-ounce) cans red	1¼	teaspoons Tabasco
	kidney beans, drained		sauce
	and rinsed	4	cups spaghetti sauce
2	(14½-ounce) cans white	1	cup macaroni noodles
	kidney beans, drained		
	and rinsed		

A very hearty soup.

In a large pot, sauté beef, onion, and garlic in oil for 5 minutes or until meat is no longer pink. Add celery, carrots, and tomatoes. Simmer 10 minutes. Add remaining ingredients. Bring to boil, reduce heat, and simmer 10 minutes until macaroni is done. Season to taste with salt and pepper.

Serve with your favorite crusty bread.

Yield: 1 gallon or 8 to 10 servings

Fresh Corn Chowder

3	cups corn, fresh or	1	(7-ounce) can chopped
	frozen		green chilies
4	tablespoons margarine	2	cups cream
2	medium onions, chopped	2	cups chicken broth
4	medium potatoes, cut in		salt and pepper
	¼ inch cubes		

Purée 2 cups of corn. Sauté onion in margarine until soft. Place corn, onion, potato, and broth in large stock pot. Bring to a boil and simmer 30 minutes, or until potato is soft. Add chilies, cream, salt, and pepper to taste. Simmer 10 minutes.

Yield: 6 servings

Mexican Bean Soup

4	bacon slices, diced	¼	teaspoon chili powder
¾	cup chopped onion		salt and pepper
¾	cup chopped celery	2	cups chicken broth
1	jalapeño, seeded and diced	1	(14½-ounce) can diced tomatoes
1	garlic clove, minced		grated cheese, cook's preference
1	(16-ounce) can refried beans		tortilla chips

In large pot, cook bacon until crispy. Add next 4 ingredients, cover, and cook over low heat for 10 minutes. Add beans, chili powder, salt and pepper. Stir in broth and tomatoes. Bring to a boil, reduce heat, and simmer 15 minutes. Top each serving with cheese and chips.

Yield: 4 servings

Mom's Bean Soup

1	(16-ounce) package navy beans	1	(14½-ounce) can whole tomatoes
1	cup chopped celery	1	(14½-ounce) can whole kernel corn, drained
1	large onion, chopped	1	ham bone or ham hocks
2	garlic cloves, minced	2-3	cups chopped ham

Sort and soak beans overnight in water, drain and rinse. Place beans in a large pot with just enough water to cover. Bring to a boil. Add remaining ingredients to pot. Add water as needed. Let soup simmer uncovered at least 4 to 5 hours, stirring occasionally.

Serve with cornbread.

Yield: 6 to 8 servings

"¡Salud, amor, pesetas, y tiempo para gozarlas!" (Health, love, wealth, and the time to enjoy them!)

Corn Chili

2	pounds ground beef	1	(14½-ounce) can whole kernel corn
1	medium onion, chopped		
1	bell pepper, chopped	1	teaspoon comino seed
1	(14½-ounce) can diced tomatoes		garlic to taste
			chili powder to taste
1	(10½-ounce) can cream style corn		salt and pepper to taste

A hearty, warming meal for a blue norther.

In a large pot, brown meat with onion and green pepper, drain. Add remaining ingredients and simmer 20 to 30 minutes.

Superb served over rice!

Yield: 6 servings

Golden Squash Soup

2	tablespoons butter	3	cups chicken broth
4	leeks, sliced and washed		salt and fresh ground pepper
6	cups cubed peeled butternut squash	1	cup milk

Leeks look like giant onions and have a very mild creamy taste. Use only the white and light green parts. Rinse under cool water after slicing.

Melt 1 tablespoon butter in large saucepan. Sauté leeks until soft. Stir in squash, broth, salt and pepper. Cover and simmer 30 minutes, until squash is soft. Place mixture in blender or food processor. Process until smooth. Reheat over low heat. Gently stir in milk and remaining butter. Heat through.

Yield: 6 servings

Cream of Pumpkin Soup

¼	cup finely chopped onions	1	teaspoon brown sugar
2	tablespoons butter	⅛	teaspoon nutmeg
1	teaspoon curry	¼	teaspoon salt
1	tablespoon flour	⅛	teaspoon black pepper
2	(10½-ounce) cans chicken broth	1	cup milk
1	(16-ounce) can pumpkin		chives, minced
			parsley, minced

In 3-quart saucepan, sauté onion in butter over medium heat until soft. Stir in curry and flour, cook until bubbly. Gradually stir in broth. Add pumpkin, sugar, and seasonings. Cook, stirring constantly until mixture begins to boil. Stir in milk and heat through, but do not boil. Sprinkle each serving with minced chives and parsley.

Yield: 8 servings

Gazpacho Blanco

2	large cucumbers, peeled and seeded	1	cup sour cream
1½	cups seedless green grapes	1	teaspoon salt or to taste
		½	teaspoon ground white pepper
1	medium avocado, chopped	3	cups chicken broth
1	garlic clove	3	tablespoons dry vermouth
1	cup plain yogurt		

Garnish

1½	cups seedless green grapes, halved	1	cup chopped scallions
1½	cups cubed avocado	1	cup chopped bell pepper

Cut cucumbers in 2-inch pieces. Combine with grapes, avocado, and garlic in food processor. Process a few seconds, leaving some texture. Pour in large bowl. Add yogurt and remaining ingredients. Mix well, taste, and adjust seasonings. Cover and chill overnight. Serve in bowls with a selection of garnishes.

Yield: 8 to 10 servings

An interesting twist to an ordinary gazpacho.

Orange Soup

3	cups plain yogurt	1	pinch white pepper
¾	cup cold water	½	teaspoon salt
2	oranges, peeled and segmented	1	tablespoon sugar
1	teaspoon orange zest	1	teaspoon chopped fresh mint
1	pinch cardamom		fresh mint leaves

In a large bowl, mix yogurt and water. Carefully peel membrane away from orange pulp, letting juices fall in a bowl. Combine zest, peeled segments and any juice with yogurt. Stir in next 5 ingredients. Refrigerate overnight. Stir before serving and garnish with fresh mint leaves.

Something cool for those long hot South Texas summers.

Yield: 4 servings

A cool refreshing soup from Chef Christian Chavanne previously of the Corpus Christi Yacht Club.

Cold Cream of Spinach Soup

½	cup butter	30-40	ounces fresh washed spinach, stems removed
1	medium white onion, chopped fine	½-1	teaspoons salt
2	(14½-ounce) cans chicken broth	½-1	teaspoon white pepper
		2	cups half and half

In a 5-quart stock pot, sauté onion in butter until soft. Add broth and bring to a boil. Add spinach, reduce heat and simmer covered for 20 minutes, stirring occasionally. Cool 30 minutes. In food processor or blend, process soup in small batches until smooth. Add salt and white pepper. Refrigerate soup covered 1 to 2 hours. Add half and half and return to refrigerator over night to let flavors meld.

For a thinner soup, add more half and half; to thicken, add 2 table-spoons flour and stir well.

Yield: 8 to 10 servings

¡VIVA! Tradiciones

Chicken Luncheon Sandwich

2 cups cooked, chopped chicken
4 hard boiled eggs, chopped
3 celery stalks, finely chopped
1 (10-ounce) can Mandarin oranges, drained
1 cup mayonnaise
½ cup pecan or cashew pieces
1 (12½-ounce) can pineapple rings, drained
1 loaf wheat bread
1 (8-ounce) package light cream cheese
3 tablespoons sour cream
1 (6-ounce) jar stuffed green olives, sliced
lettuce

A satisfying casual luncheon sandwich.

Cook chicken until tender and cut in bite-size pieces. Combine chicken with next 5 ingredients. Refrigerate for 2 to 3 hours. Use pineapple can to cut circles out of bread. Mix cream cheese with sour cream. Spread on bread circle. Layer bread, pineapple and chicken mixture. Top with olives.

Chicken mixture can be made the night before.

Yield: 8 to 10 sandwiches

Chicken and Artichoke Sandwich

1½ cups cooked, shredded chicken
1 (6-ounce) jar artichoke hearts, drained
1 clove garlic
¼ cup mayonnaise
2 tablespoons Dijon mustard
3 tablespoons capers
⅓ cup chopped green onions
10 slices of bread

Place chicken, artichokes, and garlic in a food processor and pulse until coarsely chopped. Mix with mayonnaise and mustard. Blend chicken mixture with capers and green onion. Serve between 2 slices of bread or hollowed out sandwich roll.

Serve with a slice of tomato, red pepper and onion.

Yield: 5 sandwiches

Grilled Veggi Melt

8	slices of bread	8	red onion rings
4	slices of Cheddar cheese	4	slices of Swiss cheese
1	cup alfalfa sprouts	4	mushrooms, sliced
1	avocado, peeled and sliced		seasoned salt
2	Roma tomatoes, sliced		butter

Butter one side of 4 slices of bread. On the other 4 slices, layer slice of Cheddar cheese, alfalfa sprouts, avocado, and tomato. Sprinkle tomato with salt. Add mushrooms, onion, Swiss cheese, and top with buttered bread slice. Brown sandwich in buttered skillet. Flip sandwich and grill other side.

Use your favorite combination of veggies.

Yield: 4 sandwiches

Spinach Mushroom Sandwich

1	package frozen chopped spinach	¼	teaspoon seasoned salt
1	pint lowfat sour cream	6	English muffins, split
¼	teaspoon nutmeg	1	cup thinly sliced mushrooms

A real healthy treat, but be careful, they are addictive!

Preheat broiler. Cook spinach and drain. Blend spinach, sour cream, nutmeg, and salt. Place spinach mixture on muffin and top with mushrooms. Broil until mushrooms are slightly browned and muffins edges are slightly crisp.

Yield: 6 sandwiches

Tomato Tea Sandwich

1	(8-ounce) package cream cheese, softened	½	cup sundried tomatoes, rehydrated
¼	cup unsalted butter, softened	1	tablespoon chopped basil
½	cup grated Parmesan cheese	1	loaf of bread

Combine all ingredients in food processor. Process until smooth. Trim crust from bread and spread with tomato mixture. Top with another bread slice and cut in triangles.

Yield: 2 dozen finger sandwiches or 2½ cups of spread

This also makes a great appetizer when served on crackers or garlic croutons.

Waldorf Sandwich

1	(8-ounce) package cream cheese, softened	1	large apple, unpeeled and diced
½	cup mayonnaise	½	cup minced celery
1	tablespoon sugar	½	cup walnuts, chopped
1	cup grated sharp Cheddar cheese	1	loaf of bread

Beat first 3 ingredients with electric mixer at medium speed until smooth. Stir in remaining ingredients. Cover and chill 1 hour. Prepare sandwiches.

Yield: 8 to 10 sandwiches

Cover sandwiches with a damp cloth to keep bread soft until ready to serve.

Dilly Egg Sandwich

½ cup mayonnaise	1 tablespoon chopped pimento
3-4 tablespoons minced fresh dill weed	1 tablespoon chopped parsley
1 teaspoon Dijon mustard	dash of salt
⅓ cup chopped celery	dash of white pepper
6 hard-boiled eggs, chopped	dash of Tabasco
	8 slices of bread

The perfect solution for leftover Easter eggs.

Combine first 4 ingredients. Mix in egg and add more mayonnaise, if necessary. Add pimento and parsley. Season with salt, pepper, and Tabasco to taste. Refrigerate 2 to 3 hours before assembling sandwiches.

Use half amount of dried dill weed, if fresh is not available.

Yield: 4 sandwiches

Teatime Cucumber Sandwiches

1 medium cucumber, peeled and seeded	3 green onions, chopped
8 ounces cream cheese, softened	8 slices of bread
½ cup sour cream	2 drops green food coloring (optional)
½ teaspoon dry mustard	parsley, finely chopped (optional)
salt and pepper	

Trim crust from bread and set aside. Finely chop cucumber and drain on paper towels. Blot to dry. Combine cream cheese, sour cream, and seasonings. Add coloring, if desired. Combine cucumbers and onions with cream cheese mixture. Spread mixture on bread and make sandwiches. Cut in rounds or triangles. Roll edges in chopped parsley if desired. Cover with damp dish towel and refrigerate until ready to serve.

Add more cream cheese if mixture is too thin.

Yield: 2 dozen finger sandwiches

Pasta and Vegetarian

Padre Island

One hundred and thirteen miles of rolling waves, steady breezes, sandy beaches, sand castles, seashells and sea creatures, make up Padre Island. Located along the South Texas Coast and bordering the Gulf of Mexico, it is one of the most impressive natural regional attractions. Whether you are looking for an all-but-deserted stretch of beach for your private amusement or a more populated area for seaside gaming, the island beaches of the Coastal Bend offer it all. At almost seventy miles long, Padre Island National Seashore is the largest undeveloped barrier island in the continental United States. It varies in width from a few hundred yards to three miles. On it are varying environments, including stable dunes and dunes being formed by wind-blown sand, expanses of grasslands, shelled beaches and pure sand beaches that slope toward the water. Hundreds of thousands of tourists visit the area each year. For anyone willing to hike or drive in the deep white sand, this stretch of beach offers plenty of room for solitary appreciation. The National Seashore is not the only place to play in soft sand or chase the surf of the Coastal Bend shoreline, for many county parks offer plenty of opportunities to windsurf, fish, sail, jet-ski, throw beach balls or just lie back and absorb the sunshine. From the piers, a fishing line may snag black drum, speckled trout, redfish, flounder, pompano, and even a hammerhead shark. The wealth of life and beauty belies the danger that has become a fact of life along the Gulf Coast and the history of the seashore is marked by the unforgettable effects of the most catastrophic of storms, the hurricane. Before the seawall and breakwater were built in Corpus Christi Bay, the developing city was devastated by the great storm of 1919, which brought flooding rain, waves, lightning and raging winds. Later came hurricanes Carla and Beulah in 1967. The area's most recent big storms have been Celia in 1970 and Allen in 1980. Though horrible experiences, their strengths have never doused the spirits of the residents who are addicted to the enchanted shore line.

¡VIVA! Tradiciones

Tortellini with Sundried Tomatoes, Spinach, and Pine Nuts

1   (12-ounce) package cheese tortellini
½   cup pine nuts
1   cup sundried tomatoes
3   tablespoons olive oil

1   (10-ounce) bag spinach, washed and steamed
½   cup Parmesan cheese
salt and pepper to taste

Cook pasta according to package directions. Drain. Toast pine nuts in oven until lightly browned. Rehydrate sundried tomatoes with boiling water and chop into 3 or 4 pieces. Heat oil in skillet, add spinach, and cook for 3 minutes or until wilted. Add tomatoes and mix well. Spoon over pasta. Add nuts and toss well. Sprinkle with Parmesan cheese and serve.

Yield: 4 main course servings

Pinenuts or pignoli lend a wonderful toasted flavor to this dish.

Pasta ai Asparagi

2   pounds asparagus, cleaned and trimmed
2   tablespoons butter
2   tablespoons olive oil
1   clove garlic, minced
3   Roma tomatoes, seeded and diced

3   tablespoons heavy cream
salt and pepper to taste
1   pound linguini, cooked al dente and drained
2   tablespoons Parmesan cheese

Cut asparagus diagonally into 1-inch long pieces and sauté in butter, oil, and garlic for 3 minutes. Add tomatoes and simmer on low heat for 2 minutes. Stir cream into mixture. Season with salt and pepper. Toss sauce with hot linguini and sprinkle with Parmesan cheese. Serve immediately.

Yield: 4 to 6 main course servings

Janie's Basil Lasagne

½	pound lasagne noodles, cooked al dente, drained, and rinsed	1	egg
		½	cup Parmesan cheese
½	cup pesto	½	pound Mozzarella cheese, grated
1	cup Ricotta cheese		

Garnish with slices of fresh Roma tomatoes and basil leaves.

Combine pesto, Ricotta, egg, and Parmesan cheese until well blended. Grease a 9x13 baking dish. Place one layer of lasagne noodles in dish and cover with Ricotta/pesto mixture. Place a second layer of lasagne noodles and spread Mozzarella cheese. Sprinkle with Parmesan cheese. Bake uncovered at 350° for 25 minutes.

Yield: 6 main course servings

Vegetarian Power Pasta

1	tablespoon virgin olive oil	½	cup dry white wine
		1½	cups chicken broth, heated
3	green onions, chopped		
2	carrots, sliced	1	head broccoli, cut into florets
1	tablespoon fresh, chopped ginger		
		1	tablespoon cornstarch
½	teaspoon dried basil	3	tablespoons cold water
½	red pepper, seeded and sliced	1	(12-ounce) package pasta, cooked
½	yellow pepper, seeded and sliced	salt and pepper to taste	

Use your favorite pasta or whatever happens to be in the pantry.

Sauté onions and carrots for 3 minutes in olive oil. Add ginger, basil, peppers, and wine; cook for 3 minutes. Add broth and broccoli. Cook for 4 minutes. Dissolve cornstarch in cold water and stir into vegetable mixture. Cook until slightly thickened. Season to taste. Pour over pasta and serve hot.

Yield: 4 main course servings

Vegetable Lasagne

1 (12-ounce) package lasagne noodles, cooked al dente, drained, and rinsed
4 tablespoons olive oil
5 cloves garlic, chopped
⅓ cup chopped onion
2 medium carrots, sliced thin
8 ounces fresh mushrooms, sliced
1 (10-ounce) package frozen spinach, thawed and drained
2 tablespoons fresh basil, or 1 tablespoon dried
1 tablespoon dried oregano
2 (15-ounce) cans diced tomatoes
2 tablespoons lemon juice
2 (15-ounce) containers cottage cheese
2 eggs
1 cup Parmesan cheese
2 cups grated Mozzarella cheese

Sauté 3 cloves garlic and onion in 2 tablespoons olive oil until tender. Add carrots and cook 5 minutes. Add mushrooms and spinach and warm through. In a medium saucepan, heat 2 tablespoons olive oil and sauté remaining 2 cloves garlic, basil, and oregano until tender. Add tomatoes and simmer 10 minutes. Add lemon juice. Place cottage cheese in blender and process until smooth. Add eggs and half cup Parmesan cheese. Pulse until mixed. In a greased 9x13-inch casserole, place 1 layer of noodles, ⅓ of vegetables, ⅓ of cottage cheese mixture, one-third of tomato sauce, and ⅓ of grated Mozzarella. Repeat layers. Bake uncovered at 400° for 30 to 40 minutes.

Yield: 8 main course servings

Pesto Genovesa

2½ cups fresh basil leaves, rinsed and patted dry
2 large cloves garlic, chopped
½ cup walnuts or pine nuts
½ cup olive oil
¼ cup Parmesan cheese
¼ cup grated Romano cheese
salt and pepper to taste

Process basil, garlic, and walnuts in food processor or blender. Add oil in slow steady stream while processor is running. Turn off and add cheeses, salt and pepper. Process briefly to combine.

The oil and gas industry opened up in 1914, boomed in the 1930's, and remains today a powerful economic South Texas influence.

Linguine Florentine

2	pounds fresh spinach	½	teaspoon pepper
4	ounces linguine	1	tablespoon chopped
2	teaspoons olive oil		walnuts
½	cup Parmesan cheese		

Remove stems from spinach, wash leaves thoroughly and dry. Sauté spinach in non-stick skillet for 3 minutes or until wilted and tender. Finely chop leaves, and set aside. Cook linguine according to package directions. Drain and combine linguine with oil, tossing gently. Add spinach, cheese, and pepper and toss gently. Sprinkle with walnuts and serve.

Yield: 2 servings

Fresh Parmesan cheese cannot be beat. Once you have tried shaving your own you will never go back to the can.

Tomato and Basil Pasta

2	tablespoons olive oil	3	artichoke hearts, quartered
⅔	cup diced green onions	1	tablespoon capers
1	clove garlic, minced	12	ounces angel hair pasta, cooked
3	Roma tomatoes, chopped		
½	cup dry white wine		Parmesan cheese to taste
3	ounces black olives, sliced	½	cup pine nuts, toasted
¼	cup chopped fresh basil		

Sauté scallions and garlic in oil for 2 minutes. Add tomatoes and wine and cook for 1 minute. Add remaining ingredients except pasta and cook for 2 minutes. Toss with cooked pasta and top with Parmesan cheese and pine nuts if desired.

Yield: 4 main course servings

Basil used to be considered a precious herb available only to the very rich. Now it is found growing in most backyard gardens.

Linguine with Broccoli and Cauliflower

1	cup Ricotta cheese	1	cup olive oil
1/3	cup grated Romano cheese	6	cloves garlic, minced
1	teaspoon salt	1	pound mushrooms, sliced thick
1	medium head cauliflower, cut into florets	2	teaspoons salt
1	bunch fresh broccoli, trimmed and cut into florets	½	teaspoon red pepper flakes, crushed
		1	pound linguine
			Romano cheese, grated

Combine Ricotta and Romano cheese and set aside. Boil cauliflower and broccoli in lightly salted water until crisp tender. Remove vegetables with slotted spoon and reserve liquid. Sauté garlic in olive oil until lightly browned. Add mushrooms, salt, and red pepper; sauté about 5 minutes. Stir in broccoli and cauliflower and cook for 10 minutes. If mixture gets too dry, add some of reserved cooking liquid. Bring reserved liquid to a boil, add linguine, and cook al dente, about 10 to 12 minutes. Drain. Toss hot pasta, hot vegetable sauce, and cheese mixture. Serve with additional Romano cheese, if desired.

Vegetable mixture can be made ahead and reheated later.

Yield: 8 main course servings

The Corpus Christi Naval Air Station was built in 1941 as a naval air training facility. The location was ideal because the prevailing breeze was favorable for landings most of the year. It was once the largest naval flight training center in the world and continues to train many pilots today.

Divine Wisdom Fettucine

1	(8-ounce) package cream cheese	1	(16-ounce) package fresh fettucine, cooked and drained
½	cup butter or margarine		parsley, minced
1	(12-ounce) can evaporated milk		cracked pepper
½	cup freshly grated Parmesan cheese		

In a double boiler melt butter and cream cheese together. Stir in canned milk and whisk until creamy. Add ¼ cup Parmesan cheese and minced parsley. Toss warm fettucine into sauce. Serve immediately with cracked pepper and more Parmesan cheese if desired.

Yield: 4 to 6 main course servings

If counting calories, use light cream cheese and evaporated skim milk. Add diced ham, chicken, shrimp, green peas, black olives, or mushrooms for a heartier one dish meal.

Fantastic with chicken or seafood.

Speckels' Smoked Gouda Pasta

1 pound fresh asparagus (tips only)
1 (8-ounce) package fresh mushrooms, chopped
1 medium sweet onion (1015 or Vidalia), chopped
2 carrots, thinly sliced
¼ cup olive oil
½ cup canola oil
½ cup chicken broth
salt and pepper to taste
1 (8-ounce) package angel hair pasta, cooked al dente
1 cup grated smoked Gouda cheese

Sauté vegetables in olive oil, set aside, and keep warm. Mix canola oil and chicken stock and beat until thick. Salt and pepper to taste. Toss with vegetables, hot pasta, and cheese using just enough sauce to coat pasta. If any sauce is left over, refrigerate and use again later.

Yield: 4 side course servings

Cherry's Linguine

3 cloves garlic, crushed
½ cup chopped fresh basil
½ cup extra virgin olive oil
6 Roma tomatoes, chopped
2 teaspoons salt
1 teaspoon pepper
1 pound Brie or light cream cheese, chopped into cubes
1½ pounds linguine, broken, cooked and drained

Olive oil is actually a fruit juice that can vary greatly by the olives used.

Combine first 6 ingredients and let sit at room temperature for 3 hours. Place cheese in a large pasta or serving bowl. Top with hot pasta and garlic/basil mixture, and toss. Serve immediately.

Yield: 6 main course servings

Pasta Alla Puttanesca

tablespoons olive oil	**1 (12-ounce) package angel**
garlic cloves, minced	**hair pasta, cooked al**
(2-ounce) can chopped	**dente and drained**
black olives	**⅓ cup chopped parsley**
tablespoons small capers	**½ tablespoon ground**
large tomatoes, chopped	**pepper**
anchovy fillets, rinsed	**Parmesan cheese**
and chopped	

Sauté garlic, olives, capers, tomatoes, and anchovies in olive oil for 3 minutes. Add pasta and toss. Sprinkle with pepper and toss again. Top with parsley and cheese; serve immediately.

An ancient, classic Italian recipe.

Yield: 2 main course servings

Sonora Casserole

cups tomato sauce	**3 cups zucchini, steamed**
½ teaspoon ground cumin	**1 cup corn, cooked**
½ teaspoons cayenne	**1 4-ounce can diced green**
pepper	**chilies**
½ tablespoons white	**¾ cup grated Cheddar**
vinegar	**cheese**
clove garlic	**¾ cup sour cream**
corn tortillas, cut into	**½ cup chopped green**
strips	**onions**
olive oil	**salt to taste**

Combine tomato sauce, cumin, cayenne pepper, vinegar, and garlic in a saucepan. Simmer 10 minutes and season to taste with salt. Heat oil in frying pan and briefly fry corn tortillas. Drain on paper towels. In a x13 baking dish layer in this order: tomato sauce, zucchini, tortilla strips, corn, green chilies, and cheese until ingredients are gone. Bake uncovered at 350° for 20 to 30 minutes. Remove from oven and top with sour cream and green onions.

Can substitute other squashes for some or all of the zucchini.

Yield: 8 main course servings

Biriyani

1	cup chopped onion		1	cup cauliflower, cut into florets
2	cloves garlic, crushed			
2½	teaspoons curry powder		½	cup currants
¾	teaspoon cinnamon		1	cup brown rice, uncooked
⅛	teaspoon ground cloves			
1	teaspoon salt		1	cup peas, frozen or fresh
2¾	cups water		1	tomato, chopped
2	carrots, thinly sliced			

Serve with cucumber and yogurt salad and pita bread.
A traditional Indian dish, spicy, yet with less than two grams of fat per serving.

In a large pan, cook onions and garlic in ¼ cup of water for 5 minutes. Add curry, cinnamon, cloves, and salt and cook for 2 minutes. Add the remaining water, carrots, cauliflower, currants, and rice. Bring to a boil, cover, reduce heat, and simmer about 40 minutes. Stir in tomatoes and peas and cook an additional 15 minutes. Serve hot.

Yield: 4 main course servings

Light Tamale Pie

2	tablespoons oil			pinch of salt
½	cup chopped green pepper			pinch of cumin
½	cup chopped red pepper		½	teaspoon oregano, crushed
1	cup finely chopped onion		½	teaspoon basil, crushed
1	teaspoon finely chopped garlic		½	teaspoon thyme, crushed
¼	cup vegetable broth		2	cups milk
¼	cup chopped green chilies		5	tablespoons yellow cornmeal
2	cups canned tomatoes, drained and diced		2	eggs, beaten
1⅔	cups canned corn		½	cup grated Cheddar cheese
2	tablespoons chili powder		½	cup grated Mozzarella cheese

Chilies vary in size, color, shape, and flavor. Generally, the smaller the chili, the hotter the fire.

Preheat oven to 350°. Coat a 9x13 pan with vegetable cooking spray. In a lightly oiled skillet, sauté peppers, onion, and garlic until soft. Add broth, chilies, tomatoes, corn and seasonings. Simmer for 10 minutes. In top of a double boiler bring milk to a simmer. Add cornmeal and stir constantly until thickened. Remove from heat and beat in eggs. Combine cornmeal mixture and vegetable mixture. Pour in prepared pan and bake 1 hour or until set. Sprinkle cheeses over top and bake 5 more minutes.

Yield: 8 main course servings

¡VIVA! Tradiciones

Chile Cheese Casserole

1½ cups Ricotta cheese
1½ cup grated Cheddar
   cheese, shredded
2 eggs
¼ cup chopped green onion
1 (4-ounce) can chopped
   green chilies, drained
4 (6-inch) corn tortillas,
   each cut into 8 wedges
¼ cup chopped bell pepper
1 clove garlic, minced

2 (16-ounce) cans red
   kidney beans, drained
   and rinsed
1 (14½-ounce) can
   tomatoes, cut into
   wedges
1 (8-ounce) tomato sauce
2 teaspoons chili powder
2 tablespoons chopped
   green onion

Green chilies are quite high in Vitamin C, with twice the amount as citrus, while dried red chilies contain more Vitamin A than carrots.

In large bowl mix Ricotta cheese, 1 cup Cheddar cheese, eggs, onion, and green chilies. Place tortillas on an ungreased baking sheet and bake at 350° for 10 minutes, or until crisp. In a large skillet sauté bell pepper and garlic until tender. Stir in beans, tomatoes, tomato sauce, and chili powder. Bring to boil, reduce heat, and simmer uncovered for 5 minutes, stirring occasionally. Place ⅓ of tortilla wedges in bottom of a well greased 2-quart casserole dish. Spread half of the Ricotta mixture on tortillas. Next, layer half of bean mixture. Repeat layers reserving ⅓ of tortillas. Cover and bake at 350° for 30 minutes. Sprinkle with remaining cheese and bake uncovered for an additional 5 minutes or until cheese melts. Garnish with green onions and serve with remaining tortilla wedges.

Yield: 8 main course servings

Classic Cheese Enchiladas

Sauce

2	tablespoons vegetable oil
1	medium onion, chopped
2	cloves garlic, crushed
2	(14½-ounce) cans whole tomatoes, broken up

1	tablespoon chili powder
½	teaspoon cumin
¼	teaspoon oregano
1	teaspoon salt

Enchiladas

	oil for frying tortillas
24	corn tortillas
2	medium onions, chopped

1½	pounds Colby or Monterey Jack cheese (or combination), grated

For chili con carne sauce: brown ½ pound ground meat with onion and garlic. Finish sauce as directed.

To prepare sauce, sauté onion and garlic in oil. Add remaining 5 ingredients, cover, and simmer for 30 minutes. Purée in blender for a smooth sauce. Heat oil in a 10-inch skillet over medium heat. With tongs, dip each tortilla in the oil until softened, approximately 5 seconds. Place on a paper towel to drain. Fill each tortilla with a heaping tablespoon of cheese and one-half tablespoon onion. Roll and place seam side down in a greased 9x13 casserole. Pour enchilada sauce over tortillas and top with remaining cheese. Bake uncovered at 350° for 20 to 30 minutes.

Yield: 8 main course servings

Tangy Tomato Pie

1	(9-inch) pie shell, unbaked
	sprinkle of dried basil
3	medium tomatoes, peeled and sliced
¾	cup mayonnaise
1	cup grated Cheddar cheese

1	(4-ounce) can sliced mushrooms, drained
1	teaspoon chopped green onions
1	teaspoon finely chopped green pepper

A few dashes of cayenne or Tabasco will give this a little kick!

Sprinkle pie shell with basil, prick and bake 10 minutes until lightly browned. Arrange half tomato slices in pie shell. Combine mayonnaise and next 4 ingredients. Spread half of the mayonnaise mixture over the tomatoes and repeat layers. Bake at 350° for 35 minutes.

Yield: 6 main course servings

Lentil Tomato Bake

2	cups cooked lentils	½	cup chopped mushrooms
2	cups tomato sauce	½	teaspoon garlic powder
½	cup chopped onion	¼	teaspoon Italian
½	cup chopped celery		seasoning
1	tablespoon Dijon mustard	¼	teaspoon celery seed
1	cup rolled oats		salt and pepper to taste

Mix ingredients in order listed and spoon into loaf pan lightly coated with vegetable cooking spray. Bake uncovered at 350° for 45 minutes. Let stand 5 minutes. Invert on to a platter, garnish as desired and serve.

Yield: 6 main course servings

Cilantro Pesto

3	cloves garlic	2	jalapeños, chopped and seeded
½	cup chopped cilantro	⅓	cup Parmesan cheese
½	cup chopped basil	½	cup chopped pecans
¼	cup chopped sundried tomatoes	½	cup olive oil

Pulse first 5 ingredients in a food processor. Add cheese and pecans; pulse again. Slowly add oil until pesto is smooth.

Toss with cooked pasta of your choice. Also wonderful spread on slices of French bread and broiled.

Pesto, meaning a paste ground in a mortar with a pestle, can be stored in the freezer for up to one year. Try freezing pesto in ice cube trays. A very convenient way to use only what you need.

Sun-dried Tomato and Olive Pesto

⅔　cup oil-packed sun-dried
　　tomatoes
　　olive oil
¾　cup packed, stemmed
　　fresh parsley
⅔　cup canned black olives,
　　drained

½　cup pine nuts
2　shallots, coarsely
　　chopped
2　garlic cloves
1　tablespoon red wine
　　vinegar

Strain tomatoes into a glass measuring cup. Pour in enough olive oil measure one-fourth cup. In food processor, chop drained tomatoes and next 6 ingredients. With machine running, gradually add ¼ cup reserved oil and process until mixture is well blended. If too dry, add olive oil by spoonfuls. Season with salt and pepper. Cover and refrigerate for 2 days or freeze for 1 week. Bring to room temperature before tossing with your favorite hot pasta.

Yield: 2 cups

¡VIVA! Tradiciones

THE JUNIOR LEAGUE of Corpus Christi

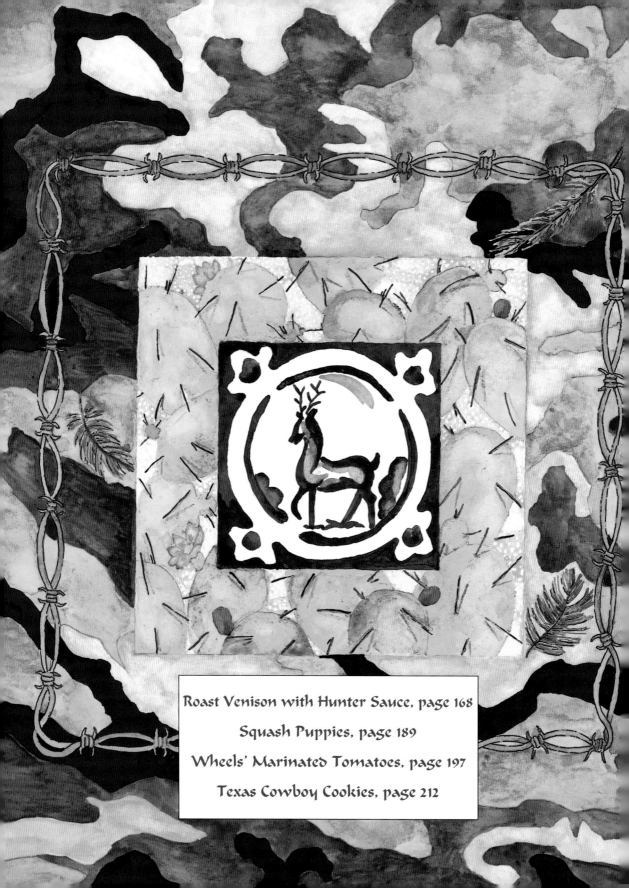

Seafood

Corpus Christi Bay

As a showcase for main attractions, from wild life and sport to the arts and commerce, Corpus Christi Bay is a focal point of life in the Coastal Bend. Before the sun rises, as its spotlight, local shrimpers start their rigs and go in search of the best spots for throwing their nets, waking the ubiquitous gulls that will follow them, waiting for catches of their own. Later, with much of the shrimp packed for delivery to supermarkets and restaurants, some shrimpers will dock their boats and sell the freshly caught seafood to patrons and tourists at the marina. More over, many other varieties including oysters, crab and flounder are harvested from the Gulf waters. The tides are mild and water temperatures range from 52 degrees in the coldest days of winter, usually in January, to 85 degrees during the long, almost tropical summers. In its perfect setting for hundreds of species of sea creatures, from huge tarpon trophy fish to Kemp's ridley sea turtles to brown pelicans. Port Aransas, formerly, "Tarpon", is even known to United States presidents as the place to fish. Salt-water fishing is a pastime to many South Texans and to the thousands of tourists who travel here annually in search of the prize winning catch. As important as the seafood, fishing and tourist industries are, the Port of Corpus Christi constitutes a larger part of the economy for other reasons. Tankers with oil products from around the world carry their loads in and out of the port, which also serves as a major link in the distribution system for the strong South Texas agricultural market. These industries mean the bay is worth hundreds of millions of dollars to the regional economy. The Bay also serves as a place for sheer enjoyment. Dining in waterfront restaurants, afternoons of sailing, sunning on the beach or touring the port aboard the Captain Clark Flagship. It is also the setting for cultural attractions, including museums, historic districts and more notably, Los Barcos, the replicas of the Columbus fleet and many privately owned yachts and sailboats.

¡VIVA! Tradiciones

Baked Stuffed Shrimp

2	pounds large shrimp, deheaded	1	bell pepper, finely chopped
5	tablespoons butter, divided	1	cup soft bread crumbs
2	tablespoons shallots, minced	1	teaspoon salt
		½	teaspoon pepper
¼	cup minced onion	1	egg, beaten
			parsley sprigs

Devein and completely shell 6 shrimp. Devein and shell remaining shrimp leaving tails on. Set aside. Sauté first 6 shrimp in 3 tablespoons butter until pink. Remove and chop finely. Sauté shallots, onions, and bell pepper in same pan for 3 to 4 minutes. Remove from heat. Stir in bread crumbs, chopped shrimp, salt and pepper. Blend in beaten egg. Set stuffing aside. Butterfly shrimp. Place shrimp in greased shallow baking dish with tails turned up. Mound 1 tablespoon stuffing in hollow of each shrimp. Drizzle remaining butter, melted over each shrimp. Bake at 400° for 10 to 12 minutes. Remove to serving platter and garnish with parsley.

Red bell pepper may be used in place of green.

Yield: 6 main course servings

Shrimp Pascal

3	pounds shrimp, peeled and deveined	1	teaspoon thyme
1	cup margarine	2	teaspoons celery salt
1	teaspoon olive oil	1	teaspoon salt
½	teaspoon Worcestershire sauce	1½	teaspoons pepper
		2	tablespoons garlic, chopped
½	teaspoon cayenne pepper	1	teaspoon rosemary

To butterfly shrimp: hold down shrimp on cutting board, back side up. Slice down the length, but not through the shrimp. Spread and flatten to form butterfly shape.

Place shrimp in a large shallow baking dish. Melt margarine with olive oil in large skillet. Add all remaining ingredients and sauté for 1 minute. Pour over shrimp and refrigerate for 6 hours. Bake at 425° for 25 minutes. Serve with lots of crusty French bread for dipping in extra sauce.

Yield: 6 main course servings

Shrimp Mezcal

1	pound shrimp, peeled and deveined			juice of 1 lime
4	tablespoons butter		1	tablespoon bottled green jalapeño sauce
1	teaspoon minced garlic		2	tomatoes, chopped
1	ounce Mezcal or tequila		¼	cup chopped cilantro
1	avocado, diced			

Sauté shrimp in butter for 1 minute. Add garlic and tequila and ignite with a match. As flame burns down, add remaining ingredients. Simmer 3 minutes, until shrimp is pink. Garnish with tomatoes and cilantro leaves. Serve immediately.

Yield: 2 servings

A spicy combination of shrimp and tequila from chef Christian Chavanne of the Corpus Christi Yacht Club.

Shrimp La Pesca

12	jumbo shrimp, peeled and butterflied		1	cup milk
1	cup chopped pecans		⅓	cup olive oil
2	cups flour, divided		3	tablespoons La Pesca butter
2	eggs			

Process pecans and 1 cup flour in food processor 1 minute. In shallow bowl, whisk together eggs and milk. Dredge each shrimp in remaining flour, dip in egg mixture and then in pecan mixture. Heat olive oil in non-stick skillet over medium heat. Add breaded shrimp and cook until golden brown, turning once. Drain off excess oil. Drizzle with melted La Pesca butter and serve immediately.

Yield: 2 servings

This South Texas version of fried shrimp comes from La Pesca Catering, chef Paul Grissom.

La Pesca Butter

⅓	cup chopped cilantro		1	tablespoon ground cumin
⅓	cup chopped parsley		½	teaspoon salt
2	arbole chilies, seeded		1	pound butter, softened

Process first 5 ingredients in food processor until minced fine. Combine butter and spices in bowl and mix well. Shape butter in a tube and wrap in plastic. Refrigerate or freeze. When ready to serve, slice in thin rounds.

¡VIVA! Tradiciones

Shrimp and Mango

2   pounds medium shrimp, peeled

4   tablespoons lemon juice, divided

4   tablespoons basil, divided

1   jalapeño, seeded and chopped

salt and pepper to taste

1   ripe mango, peeled and pitted

1   tablespoons butter

2   tablespoons olive oil

1   large red bell pepper, seeded and cut in strips

2   cloves garlic, minced

Combine shrimp, 2 tablespoons lemon juice, 2 tablespoons basil, jalapeño, salt and pepper. Stir well. Let stand 15 minutes. Cut mango in ½-inch cubes and place in small bowl. Toss gently with remaining lemon juice. In large skillet, sauté red pepper in butter and oil for 1 minute. Add shrimp with marinade, mango and garlic. Sauté 5 minutes or until shrimp turn pink. Sprinkle with remaining basil and season to taste with salt and pepper.

Yield: 4 main course servings

From 1½-pounds of fresh deheaded unpeeled shrimp you will get ¾ pound or 2 cups of peeled, deveined and cooked shrimp.

Party Paella

   whole chicken, cut up

   (8-ounce) link sausage, sliced

   medium onion, chopped

   red bell pepper, chopped

   bell pepper, chopped

   cloves garlic, chopped

½   cups long grain rice

   medium tomatoes, chopped

¼   teaspoon saffron powder

2   teaspoons salt

1   can chicken broth

1   can whole clams, drained

1½   pounds cherrystone clams in shells, scrubbed

1½   pounds shrimp, shelled

½   cup frozen peas, thawed

Season chicken with salt and pepper. Brown sausage and chicken in large skillet. Remove from pan and set aside. In same pan, sauté onion, red and green pepper and garlic until soft. Add rice, chopped tomatoes, saffron and salt. Stir in chicken broth and ½ cup water. Bring to boil. Stir in cooked sausage and canned clams. Place mixture in -quart casserole dish. Arrange chicken on top and bake at 375° for 30 minutes. Place whole clams in pan with 1-inch of boiling water. Cover and cook for 3 to 5 minutes, until clams open. Drain and discard any unopened clams. Arrange clams, shrimp, and peas on rice mixture. Bake covered for 15 minutes.

Yield: 6 to 8 main course servings

Saffron is a top shelf spice. Don't be put off by its high price because a pinch will uniquely flavor your dish.

Sin-Free Scampi

1	cup chicken broth	3	tablespoons lemon juice
2	cloves garlic, chopped	1	pound shrimp, peeled,
4	tablespoons chopped		tails left on
	shallots, divided	½	pound angel hair pasta,
4	tablespoons chopped		cooked according to
	fresh parsley, divided		package directions
¾	cup white wine		salt and pepper to taste

Combine broth, garlic, and 3 tablespoons each of shallots and parsley in a large sauce pan. Simmer for 2 minutes. Add wine and lemon juice. Cook 4 minutes or until liquid is reduced by half. Add shrimp and cook 3 to 4 minutes, until pink. Add remaining shallots and season to taste with salt and pepper. Serve over drained pasta divided evenly on 4 plates. Sprinkle with remaining parsley. Serve immediately.

Yield: 4 main course servings

Shrimp and Crab Supreme

1	onion, sliced	8	tablespoons butter
1	teaspoon dried dill weed	¼	cup flour
2	bay leaves	2	cups half and half
6	peppercorns	1	clove garlic, chopped
6	cups water	2	tablespoons
2	pounds shrimp		Worcestershire sauce
2	(10-ounce) packages	¼	teaspoon Tabasco
	frozen chopped spinach	¼	teaspoon paprika
3	tablespoons grated onion	1	tablespoon sherry
2	tablespoons lemon juice	12	ounces fresh or frozen
	salt and pepper		lump crab meat
	cayenne pepper		grated Parmesan cheese

Combine first 5 ingredients in large pot and bring to boil. Add shrimp and boil 4 to 5 minutes. Drain and cool. Shell and set aside. Cook spinach, drain and squeeze out water. Combine spinach with grated onion, lemon juice, salt and peppers. In another pan, over low heat, melt butter and add flour, stirring constantly. Slowly stir in half and half and cook until thickened. Add garlic, Worcestershire, Tabasco, paprika, and sherry. In shallow casserole, layer shrimp, crab, spinach, and cream sauce alternately. Generously sprinkle Parmesan cheese over top. Heat at 325° for 30 minutes.

An unforgettable dish.

Yield: 6 to 8 servings

Scallop Supreme

pound large sea scallops	½ cup butter, divided
flour seasoned with salt and pepper	3 cloves garlic, minced
⅓ cup olive oil	½ cup half and half
egg yolk	1 tablespoon chives
juice of 1 lemon	1 tablespoon parsley
	Parmesan cheese

Dredge scallops in seasoned flour. Sauté scallops in oil over medium heat, about 4 minutes per side, turning gently. Remove to serving dish and keep warm. In separate pan, whisk egg yolk and lemon juice. Add ¼ cup butter and garlic and cook over low heat until butter is melted. Add half and half and remaining butter and stir until sauce thickens. Remove from heat and stir in chives and parsley. Pour sauce over scallops, sprinkle with Parmesan cheese and serve with crusty bread.
Very rich!

Yield: 4 servings

Shrimp Creole Mon Cher

tablespoons margarine	salt to taste
2 large onion, minced	cayenne pepper to taste
stalks celery, chopped	1 (6-ounce) can tomato paste
2 large bell pepper, chopped	1 (14½-ounce) can chopped tomatoes
tablespoons flour	3 cups water
bay leaf	2 cups shrimp, peeled
dash Tabasco	3 cups cooked white rice
dash Worcestershire sauce	

In large skillet, sauté onion, celery, and bell pepper in margarine until tender. Blend in flour. Stir in bay leaf, seasonings, tomato paste, tomatoes, and water. Simmer uncovered 30 to 40 minutes, stirring occasionally. Add shrimp and simmer an additional 10 minutes. Remove bay leaf and serve with rice.

Yield: 6 servings

Shrimp Creole for the family. Quick and easy, just in time for supper.

Gulf Coast Jambalaya

¼	cup olive oil	1	tablespoon chopped fresh cilantro
¾	cup smoked ham	1	teaspoon thyme
⅔	cup andouille sausage	3	bay leaves
2	cups chopped onion	1	teaspoon ground cumin
6	scallions, chopped	1	teaspoon cayenne pepper
6	cloves garlic, chopped	3	cups fish or chicken stock
1	large bell pepper, seeded and chopped	3	cups uncooked rice
1	large red bell pepper, seeded and chopped	24	medium shrimp, peeled and deveined
6	stalks celery, chopped	24	fresh oysters with liquor
8	large tomatoes, peeled, seeded, and chopped	8	ounces crab meat
1	tablespoon oregano		salt and pepper
2	teaspoons basil		

Preheat oven to 350°. In large skillet, sauté ham and sausage in oil for 6 to 8 minutes, until crisp. Add onion and next 5 ingredients; sauté 5 minutes. Add tomatoes and seasonings and cook 5 minutes more. Add stock and rice and bring to boil. Remove from heat. Pour mixture in a large baking dish, cover, and bake 15 minutes. Add shrimp, oysters with liquor, and crabmeat. Cover and bake for 15 minutes more. Remove bay leaves. Season with salt and pepper and serve immediately.

An oyster's natural juices are referred to as "liquor."

Yield: 10 main course servings

Across the Corpus Christi Bay is Port Aransas where the game fishing boats leave for Gulf waters in search of tarpon, marlin, and mackerel.

Fish Marinara

1	tablespoon olive oil	4	fish filets
2	cloves garlic, minced	8	ounces spaghetti, cooked and drained
3	tomatoes, chopped	½	cup Parmesan cheese
1	teaspoon oregano		
	salt and pepper		

In large deep skillet, sauté garlic in olive oil. Gradually add tomatoes and oregano. Season fish with salt and pepper and place in skillet. Cover and cook until fish flakes easily. Serve sauce over hot pasta and top with Parmesan cheese.

Yield: 2 to 4 servings (depends on size of fish)

The speckled trout is one of the most sought after bay fish along the Texas coast.

Seafood Enchiladas

Enchiladas
½ onion, chopped
2 cloves garlic, chopped
½ red bell pepper, diced
½ bell pepper, diced
2 tablespoons oil
½ pound fish (drum,
    redfish, or red snapper)

½ pound shrimp, peeled
    and chopped
½ pound bay scallops
1 cup chopped tomato
salt and pepper to taste
½ cup grated Monterey
    Jack cheese
12 corn tortillas

Tomatillo Sauce
2 cloves garlic, minced
½ onion, chopped
1 tablespoon vegetable oil
2 jalapeños, seeded
2 serrano peppers, seeded

10 tomatillos, husks
    removed
1 cup chicken broth
1 tablespoon cilantro,
    chopped

This is a colorful change of pace for enchiladas. Serve with your favorite Spanish rice and black beans.

In medium skillet, sauté onion and next 3 ingredients in oil until soft. Add fish and cook over medium heat for 1 minute. Add shrimp, scallops and tomato; cook until shrimp turn pink, about 5 minutes. Season with salt and pepper. Spray each tortilla with cooking spray and warm on griddle until soft. Fill each tortilla with filling and sprinkle with cheese. Roll and place seam-side down in 3-quart baking dish. For sauce, sauté onion and garlic in oil until tender. Place in blender with remaining ingredients, process until smooth. Pour over enchiladas and bake uncovered at 350° for 10 minutes.
For a creamy sauce, add 8-ounces sour cream before baking.

Yield: 6 main course servings

Snapper with Herb Crust

   snapper filets
¼ cup olive oil
½ loaf French bread, cubed
2 strips cooked crispy
    bacon

2 teaspoons dried basil
2 teaspoons chopped
    chives
2 teaspoons dried parsley

Coat fish with oil. Process remaining ingredients in food processor until crumbly. Roll fish in bread mixture. Place in oiled baking dish. Bake at 400° for 15 minutes.

Yield: 6 main course servings

Herbs love to be touched. Touching will release the aroma, the best reason for growing them.

Jarlsberg Shrimp

1	onion, chopped	1	(8-ounce) package cream
1	bell pepper, chopped		cheese, cubed
2	stalks celery, chopped	¼	teaspoon cayenne
2	cloves garlic, chopped		pepper
½	pound mushrooms, thinly	3	cups cooked rice
	sliced	2	pounds shrimp, cooked
4	tablespoons butter		and peeled
1	tablespoons flour	2	cups grated Jarlsberg
1	cup milk		cheese

In large skillet, sauté first 5 ingredients in butter until tender. Stir in flour and simmer to a thick paste. Add milk and whisk until smooth. Remove from heat. Add cream cheese and stir until melted. Add cayenne and rice. Mix well. Layer half rice mixture in shallow baking dish. Layer shrimp and then remaining rice mixture. Top with cheese. Bake at 350° for 25 minutes.

Recipe is successful using lowfat products.

Yield: 6 to 8 servings

Located on North Beach, the Texas State Aquarium is the largest salt water aquarium in this region. It houses unique exhibits featuring the sea life in the Gulf of Mexico.

Shrimp Ragoût

2	tablespoons butter	1	(10¾-ounce) can cream
1	onion, chopped		of mushroom soup
2	stalks celery, chopped	1	can vegetable broth
1	bell pepper, chopped	3	cups cooked rice
1	pound shrimp, peeled		salt and pepper to taste
	and deveined	½	cup toasted bread
1	(10-ounce) can tomatoes		crumbs
	and green chilies		

Sauté onions, celery, and bell pepper in butter until soft. Add shrimp and tomatoes. Simmer 5 minutes. Add soup and broth and mix well. Season with salt and pepper. Simmer another 5 minutes. Add rice and mix well. Pour into greased 3-quart baking dish. Top with bread crumbs. Bake at 400° for 20 minutes.

Tired of the same old chicken casserole, this is the answer.

Yield: 6 servings

Grilled Fish Vera Cruz

Vera Cruz Topping

1 avocado, peeled and diced	½ teaspoon salt
1 tomato, seeded, and diced	pepper to taste
¼ cup chopped green onion	6 dashes hot sauce
	2 tablespoons lemon juice
	2 teaspoons vegetable oil

Fish

2 fresh fish filets	3 tablespoons minced parsley
¼ cup olive oil	1 tablespoon cracked pepper
2 tablespoons lemon juice	
2 cloves garlic, minced	
2 tablespoons fresh chopped basil	

Combine all topping ingredients in medium bowl and refrigerate. Combine fish with remaining ingredients and marinate for 1 hour. Bake or grill over hot coals until fish flakes easily. Top with the Vera Cruz topping and serve immediately.

Wonderful served with black beans and saffron rice!

Yield: 4 main course servings

The Tarpon Inn in Port Aransas built in 1886 is a popular restored hotel which is known for housing VIP's F.D. Roosevelt and Duncan Hines.

Trout Meunière

2 pounds trout filets	½ teaspoon garlic powder
1 cup butter, melted	½ teaspoon salt
1 tablespoon Worcestershire sauce	¼ teaspoon cayenne pepper
1 cup chopped green onion tops	

Pat fish dry and place in 8x8 glass baking dish. Combine remaining ingredients in a bowl and pour over fish. Microwave on high for 5 to 6 minutes or until fish flakes easily with a fork. Halfway through cooking, rotate dish.

Garnish with parsley and lemon slices. Serve with rice.

Yield: 4 main course servings

This trout can be zapped in the microwave. But if you have not figured out how to bake in yours, simply sauté this flavorful fish in an oiled skillet.

Pescado à la Naranja

2	pounds fresh fish (red snapper, halibut, or amberjack)	1	teaspoon salt
½	cup chopped onion	½	teaspoon pepper
2	cloves garlic, minced	½	cup orange juice
2	tablespoons olive oil	1	teaspoon lemon juice
2	tablespoons chopped cilantro	1	hard boiled egg, cut into wedges

2   pounds fresh fish (red snapper, halibut, or amberjack)
½   cup chopped onion
2   cloves garlic, minced
2   tablespoons olive oil
2   tablespoons chopped cilantro

1   teaspoon salt
½   teaspoon pepper
½   cup orange juice
1   teaspoon lemon juice
1   hard boiled egg, cut into wedges
paprika
orange slices

Citrus trees are found in the backyards of many South Texas homes.

Sauté onion and garlic in oil until tender. Add cilantro, salt, and pepper Place fish in 9x13 baking dish and spread onion mixture over fish. Combine lemon and orange juices and pour over fish. Cover and bake at 400° for 20 minutes. Arrange egg slice on top of fish, sprinkle with paprika, and garnish with orange slices.

Yield: 4 to 6 main course servings

Fish Fillet Aquarium

2   tomatoes, diced
10   leaves fresh basil
3   tablespoons olive oil, divided
salt and pepper
flour

2   fish fillets (flounder, redfish, trout, etc.)
1   cup white wine
8   ounces angel hair pasta cooked al dente

A flavorful easy fish recipe that can be prepared by the novice cook. From Marco Matlolin, owner and chef of Marco's at Lamar.

Combine tomatoes, basil, and 2 tablespoons oil. Refrigerate. Season fish with salt and pepper, dust with flour. Heat remaining 1 tablespoon oil in skillet to high. Sear filets on each side. Add wine and cook until almost completely reduced. Add tomato mixture and simmer until fish is cooked through. Serve over angel hair pasta.

Yield: 2 servings

Grilled Amberjack with Sweet Pepper Relish

½	cup oil	2	cloves garlic, minced
2	tablespoons soy sauce	1	teaspoon lemon pepper
2	tablespoons dry sherry	1½	pounds amberjack or
1	teaspoon fresh grated ginger root		swordfish

Combine first 6 ingredients. Place fish and marinade in large zip top freezer bag, seal. Refrigerate 4 hours, shaking occasionally. Remove fish and reserve marinade. Grill over medium coals on oiled grill or fish basket until done, basting occasionally with marinade. Top with sweet pepper relish.

Sweet Pepper Relish

1	yellow bell pepper	3	tablespoons chopped garlic
1	red bell pepper		
⅓	cup pinenuts, toasted	1	teaspoon brown sugar
1	tablespoon olive oil		pinch ground nutmeg
1	tablespoon red wine vinegar		pinch salt
			pinch pepper

To roast peppers, char skins over gas burner or under broiler until 75% black. Place in a bag and refrigerate 15 minutes, until cool. Stem, seed, and peel peppers. Chop peppers and combine with all remaining ingredients in a small bowl. Refrigerate 2 hours.

Yield: 4 main course servings

Cajun Stuffed Snapper

4	teaspoons butter, divided
¼	cup chopped onion
3	tablespoons chopped celery
3	tablespoons chopped bell pepper
2	cloves garlic, minced
¼	cup chopped green onion
2	tablespoons minced parsley
1	cup chopped cooked shrimp
2	cups toasted bread cubes

½	cup lump crab meat, picked through
¾	teaspoon Cajun seasoning
¼	teaspoon black pepper
¼	teaspoon cayenne pepper
1	red snapper (4 pounds), pan dressed, boned, head and tail left on
	salt and pepper
¼	cup lemon juice

This dish will impress your friends. You don't have to tell them how easy it was.

Preheat oven to 450°. Lightly grease a large shallow roasting pan. Melt 2 tablespoons butter in 12-inch skillet and sauté next 4 ingredients until tender. Stir in green onions and parsley, sauté 1 minute longer. Transfer to bowl. In same skillet, melt remaining butter. Add shrimp and sauté 3 minutes. Add bread cubes, crab, Cajun seasoning and peppers. Return onion mixture to pan and mix well. Stuff cavity of fish and close with toothpicks. Place fish in prepared pan. Make several diagonal slits on fish body with sharp knife. Season with salt and pepper and lemon juice. Bake for 20 minutes or until fish flakes when tested with fork. Serve immediately.

Yield: 4 main course servings

Filets in Nut Crust

2	pounds fish filets
	salt and pepper
⅓	cup flour
1	cup bread crumbs
1	cup pecans, minced

1	egg yolk
2	egg whites
2	tablespoons water
2	tablespoons olive oil

Season fish with salt and pepper. Lightly dust with flour. Combine crumbs and nuts in bowl. Beat egg yolk and whites with water in another bowl. Heat oil in skillet. Dredge each fish portion in egg wash, then in nut mixture. Sauté fish on each side for 2 minutes or until golden. Carefully place fish in oven safe dish and bake at 350° for 10 to 20 minutes, depending on size of filets.

Yield: 4 main course servings

My Man's Favorite Fish Recipe

6	medium filets (trout, redfish, or salmon)	2	cloves garlic, minced
	salt and pepper to taste	1	teaspoon dill weed
3	tablespoons olive oil	½	teaspoon Tabasco sauce
2	tablespoons butter	2	tablespoons lemon juice
1	medium onion, chopped	½	teaspoon salt
		1	cup chopped tomatoes

Salt and pepper filets. Set aside. Sauté onion and garlic in oil and butter until soft. Add dill weed, Tabasco, lemon juice, salt and tomatoes. Simmer uncovered for 10 to 15 minutes, stirring occasionally. Grill or broil filets until fish flakes easily. Serve sauce over fish.

Yield: 4 main course servings

The Laguna Madre, which separates Corpus Christi and the entire lower Texas coast from Padre Island, boasts some of the best flounder, redfish, and pompano fishing.

Bacon-wrapped Tuna with Balsamic Glaze

Fish

2	tuna steaks, 1-inch thick		salt and pepper
8	strips bacon		

Glaze

1	tablespoon sesame seeds	⅓	cup soy sauce
½	cup balsamic vinegar	1	tablespoon honey
		3	tablespoons veal glaze

Wrap bacon around steaks and secure with toothpick. Salt and pepper generously. Grill over hot coals for 4 minutes each side. For sauce, combine all ingredients in sauce pan and reduce by half. Sauce may be refrigerated 1 week. When ready to serve, bring sauce to simmer over low heat. Whisk in 1 tablespoon butter and cook until melted. Pour sauce on plate and place fish over sauce.

A meat glaze is stock that has been reduced to a paste. It is very strong and can usually be found in paste form at most supermarkets.

An evening in Port Aransas is always worth the trip over the bridge when dining at Beulah's with chef Guy Carnathan.

Flounder Vinaigrette

4	flounder filets	¼	cup Italian vinaigrette
	paprika		salad dressing
	salt to taste	¼	cup grated Cheddar
4	slices tomato, ½ to ¾		cheese
	inch thick	1	teaspoon chopped
1	teaspoon chopped chives		parsley
¼	teaspoon dried tarragon		

Preheat oven to 475°. Arrange filets in ungreased baking dish. Sprinkle with paprika and salt. Place tomato slice on each fillet. Sprinkle with chives and tarragon. Pour dressing over filets and sprinkle with cheese. Bake uncovered until fish flakes easily, about 15 minutes. Sprinkle with parsley before serving.

Yield: 4 main course servings

On Sunday afternoons, the Corpus Christi shoreline is dotted with the bright sails of local boats and yachts out for family cruising or competitive racing.

Camp's Grilled Tuna with Yogurt Dill Sauce

Sauce

2	cups plain lowfat yogurt	¼	cup fresh dill weed,
1	tablespoon Dijon		chopped
	mustard	½	cup finely sliced green
2	teaspoons horseradish		onions
			juice of ½ lemon

Fish

2	pounds fresh tuna	¼	cup lime juice
	steaks, 1-inch thick	¼	cup olive oil

Blend all sauce ingredients. Add salt and freshly ground pepper to taste. Refrigerate. Preheat grill or broiler. Rinse steaks and pat dry. Rub steaks with lime juice, then olive oil. Broil or grill 5 to 6 minutes on each side. Serve with yogurt dill weed sauce.

Yield: 4 to 6 main course servings

¡VIVA! Tradiciones

Swiss and Crab Pie

1	cup shredded Swiss cheese	3	eggs, beaten
1	(9-inch) pastry shell, baked	1	cup half and half
¾	cup fresh crab meat	½	teaspoon lemon zest
½	cup sliced green onions, divided	¼	teaspoon dry mustard
			dash of ground mace
		¼	cup sliced almonds

Sprinkle cheese over pastry shell. Top with crab and sprinkle with ¼ cup green onions. In separate bowl combine eggs, half and half, lemon zest, mustard, and mace. Pour mixture over crab. Top with almonds and remaining green onions. Bake at 325° for 50 to 55 minutes. Remove from oven. Let cool 10 minutes before serving. Garnish with parsley.

Canned crab can be used.

Yield: 6 main course servings

Crabbin' is a popular shallow water pastime. Easier to catch than clean, crabmeat is a succulent treat.

Broiled Tuna with Rosemary

4	(4-ounce) tuna steaks	½	teaspoon dried oregano
½	cup dry white wine	¼	teaspoon salt
1	tablespoon lemon juice	⅛	teaspoon pepper
½	teaspoon garlic powder		vegetable cooking spray
1	teaspoon fresh rosemary		

Place steaks in large zip top plastic bag. Combine wine, lemon juice, and seasonings. Pour over steaks in bag, seal and refrigerate 1½ hours, turning bag occasionally. Remove steaks and discard marinade. Place steaks on greased broiler pan. Broil 3 to 4 minutes on each side or until fish flakes easily with fork.

Garnish with fresh rosemary sprigs.

Yield: 4 main course servings

Sassy Salmon Cakes with Jalapeño Mayonnaise

Jalapeño Mayonnaise
⅓	cup mayonnaise
2	teaspoons dill weed, chopped

1   teaspoon bottled green jalapeño sauce

Cakes
2   potatoes, peeled and cooked
1   (14¾-ounce) can pink salmon, drained and flaked
1   large egg
½   cup cracker crumbs, divided

1   tablespoon chopped dill weed
1   tablespoon bottled green jalapeño sauce
1   tablespoon prepared horseradish
¾   teaspoon salt
1   tablespoon butter
1   tablespoon olive oil

Combine all mayonnaise ingredients in small bowl and stir until well blended. Refrigerate. Mash potatoes. Add salmon, egg and ¼ cup cracker crumbs. Add next 4 ingredients and mix well. Place remaining cracker crumbs on small plate. Shape salmon mixture into 6 patties. Dip into crumbs coating all sides. In large skillet, heat butter and olive oil. Cook cakes 4 minutes each side. Serve with jalapeño mayonnaise.

Yield: 6 servings

Oysters Patou

½	loaf day old French bread	1	tablespoon fresh basil
1	cup margarine	6	drops Tabasco
3	medium onions, minced	1	tablespoon salt
1	medium bell pepper, chopped	2	teaspoons cayenne pepper
1	rib celery, chopped	1	teaspoon white pepper
2	cloves garlic, minced	1	teaspoon black pepper
3	pints oysters, drain and reserve liquor	1	cup sliced green onions, including tops
1	pound medium shrimp, shelled and deveined	1	cup chopped parsley
1	tablespoon fresh thyme (1 teaspoon dried)		grated Parmesan cheese

Do not be discouraged by the number of ingredients. Preparation goes much quicker than anticipated and the results are well worth the effort.

Slice bread thin and place on cookie sheet. Bake at 200° for about 30 minutes or until dried thoroughly, do not brown. Place dried bread in a bowl and pour 3 cups reserved oyster liquor; set aside to soak. Sauté onions and next 3 ingredients until soft. Add any remaining oyster liquor and cook until liquor has evaporated. Set aside 24 oysters. Cut remaining oysters in half and set aside. Cut shrimp in thirds. Add shrimp, herbs and Tabasco to vegetable mixture, cook 4 to 5 minutes. Mix salt and peppers together and add all but 1 teaspoon to pan. Add oyster halves to shrimp/vegetable mixture and cook until oysters curl around edges. Mash bread and oyster liquor. Add bread to shrimp mixture, reduce heat to low and cook until sauce is smooth. Remove from heat, add green onions and parsley. Refrigerate mixture for at least 2 hours. Arrange 24 shells or ramekins on a cookie sheet. Place one whole oyster in each shell and sprinkle with reserved salt and pepper mixture. Mound dressing over each oyster. Bake at 375° for 25 to 30 minutes. Sprinkle generously with Parmesan cheese and place under broiler to brown.

Can also be cooked in a large shallow casserole with whole oysters at bottom.

Yield: 10 to 12 servings

Beulah's Pan Fried Oysters with Shallot Cream Sauce

12	fresh oysters, shucked	2	tablespoons minced
1	cup flour		shallots
	salt and pepper	¼	cup sherry
½	cup clarified butter	1	cup heavy cream
			toast points

Clarified butter is melted butter with solids removed. It can reach higher temperatures without burning. To make: melt butter and allow solids to settle to the bottom. Skim off clear butter leaving solids undisturbed.

Dry oysters. Roll in flour seasoned with salt and pepper. Heat butter in sauté pan until very hot. Add oysters, 1 at a time and sauté quickly, turning once. Remove oysters before flour has burned. After all oysters have been cooked, add shallots and shake pan. Add sherry and flame. As fire subsides, add cream. Reduce by half, stirring constantly. Test and season as needed. Place oysters over toast points and top with sauce.

From Guy Carnathan of Beulah's in Port Aransas.

Yield: 2 servings

Crawfish Fettucine

1	onion, chopped	1	jalapeño, seeded and
2	stalks celery, chopped		chopped
1	bell pepper, seeded and	3	tablespoons parsley
	chopped	2	pounds crawfish tails,
1	clove garlic, chopped		shelled
½	cup margarine		salt and pepper to taste
⅛	cup flour		Tabasco to taste
½	cup milk	8	ounces medium egg
8	ounces Velveeta cheese,		noodles, cooked
	cubed		Parmesan cheese

Sauté onions, celery, bell pepper, and garlic in margarine. Add flour, milk and cheese. Stir until cheese is melted. Add jalapeño, parsley, and crawfish. Simmer, stirring occasionally until crawfish is cooked, about 5 minutes. Add salt, pepper and Tabasco, mix thoroughly. Pour sauce over noodles and toss. Place in 3-quart casserole dish. Sprinkle with Parmesan cheese. Cover and bake at 350° for 15 minutes.

Shrimp may be substituted for crawfish.

Yield: 6 main course servings

Poultry

Audubon and Flora and Fauna

Yellow-rumped warblers, black-bellied whistling ducks, brown boobies and winecups, bluebonnets and Indian paintbrushes. From colorful calling birds to rapturous wildflowers, wildlife flourishes in South Texas. The Coastal Bend offers one of the premier locations for bird watching in the nation, with rare sights of whooping cranes, brown pelicans, and more commonly roseate spoonbills. Tourists flock from around the world in search of the endangered whoopers, which are finally growing in number and can be watched at their winter home in the Aransas National Wildlife Refuge. The South Texas varying terrain, including sandy beaches and brush country and its temperate climates lure five hundred of America's eight hundred bird species each year. The region's importance as a stop for various flocks is recognized by its nearly twenty designated spots along the newly organized Texas Coastal Birding Trail. The 500-mile trail with ninety-six bird watching sites will help bird-watchers track grebes, white-faced ibises, and American oyster-catchers. The birds, and the tourists that follow, are attracted to the natural landscape by the vibrant colors of wildflowers, including primrose verbena, coreopsis, Texas' famous bluebonnets, and many more. Still more species of wildflowers pop up during the long hot summers and warm autumns. Strong winds, salty air and dry weather can be rough on some vegetation. Some sturdy trees that can survive the conditions best are the mesquite, live oak, soapberry and hackberry trees. The coastline boasts of the tropics with rows of palm trees bending in the ocean breezes and bougainvillea blooming in festive shades of red and pink.

¡VIVA! Tradiciones

Pollo Con Nopalitos

1	(4 pound) chicken	1	(8-ounce) can salsa ranchera
½	onion, diced		
3	cloves garlic, chopped	8	cups nopalitos, cleaned and chopped
2	tablespoons diced bell pepper		
		¼	bunch cilantro, chopped
1½	cups chicken broth		salt, pepper, and cumin powder to taste
1	(8-ounce) can tomato sauce		

Boil chicken until done; skin, bone, and cut in bite-size pieces. In a large skillet, sauté onion, garlic, and bell pepper until tender. Add tomato sauce and salsa; simmer for 5 minutes. Add chicken, nopalitos, cilantro, and seasoning. Cook for 10 minutes.

Yield: 6 to 8 servings

"Nopalitos" are the leaves from the nopal plant or the Texas Prickly Pear. Most commonly eaten steamed and mixed with scrambled eggs. They are very flavorful and are an excellent source of protein.

Chicken and Black Bean Tacos

Taco

4	boneless, skinless chicken breasts, cubed	⅓	cup chopped bell pepper
		1	jalapeño, seeded and chopped
4	tablespoons fresh lime juice, divided		
		1	teaspoon salt
2	tablespoons oil	1	tablespoon chopped fresh cilantro
4	green onions, chopped		
2	cloves garlic, minced	10	corn tortillas or taco shells
¾	cup cooked black beans		
1	cup diced fresh tomatoes		

Toppings

1	cup grated Monterey Jack cheese	1½	cups diced tomatoes
		1	cup sour cream
2	cups shredded lettuce		

In a medium saucepan, combine 2 tablespoons lime juice and oil. Sauté chicken over medium heat for 3 minutes. Remove chicken and sauté onions and garlic in same pan for 2 minutes. Add beans and next 3 ingredients; cook 2 to 3 minutes. Stir in remaining lime juice, salt, cilantro, and chicken, cook for 3 more minutes. Serve warm in tortillas with grated cheese and assorted toppings.

Serve with a bowl of Spanish rice.

Yield: 6 servings

The word "taco" in Spanish means snack. It can be a corn or flour tortilla, rolled or folded, soft or crisp-fried.

Kiko's Chicken Enchiladas de Flor Verde

1	whole chicken	1½	cups broccoli florets, blanched and chopped
3	cups chicken broth		
1	teaspoon cumin	1	cup grated Monterey Jack cheese
2	teaspoons crushed garlic		
1	teaspoon salt	1	cup sour cream
1	teaspoon paprika		vegetable oil for frying tortillas
12	corn tortillas		

This tasty version of chicken enchiladas comes from the fine folks at Kiko's Mexican Food Restaurant and Papalote Bar.

Boil chicken in lightly salted water, bone and cut in bite-size pieces. Heat broth in skillet, add chicken and spices, cook until broth is almost gone, but not dry. Dip tortillas in hot oil to soften; pat with paper towel. Fill tortillas with chicken mixture and roll. Place seam side down in shallow 3-quart baking dish. Top with any remaining chicken and broccoli. Sprinkle with cheese. Bake uncovered at 375° for 20 minutes, or until cheese melts. Top with sour cream if desired.

Yield: 6 servings

Pecan Chicken

1	cup flour	1	egg, beaten
1	cup ground pecans or pecan meal	1	cup buttermilk
		6-8	boneless, skinless chicken breast halves
¼	cup sesame seeds		
1	tablespoon paprika	⅓	cup butter, melted
1½	teaspoons salt	¼	cup coarsely chopped pecans
⅛	teaspoon pepper		

Combine flour and next 5 ingredients, set aside. In small bowl, combine egg and buttermilk. Dip chicken breasts in egg mixture and coat well with flour mixture. Place butter in 3-quart baking dish. Add breasts, turning once to coat. Sprinkle with chopped pecans and bake at 350° for 30 minutes.

Use the same recipe for fish, but reduce cooking time by half.

Yield: 8 servings

White Chili

1	pound Northern white beans, soaked and rinsed	2	teaspoons ground cumin
4	cups shredded, cooked chicken	1½	teaspoons oregano
		½	cup chopped cilantro
5	cups chicken broth, reserved or canned	¼	teaspoon cayenne pepper
2	medium onions, chopped	3	cups grated Monterey Jack cheese
2	cloves garlic, minced	2	avocados, diced
1	tablespoon oil	2	tomatoes, diced
2	(4-ounce) cans chopped green chilies	1	cup sour cream
		1	cup chopped onion

Cook beans in water for 45 minutes. Drain and set aside. Combine beans, chicken, broth, and half of chopped onion in large stockpot. Bring to a boil, reduce heat, and simmer for 3 hours. Sauté remaining onion and garlic in oil until tender; add to beans. Stir in chilies and next 4 ingredients. Simmer 1 hour, stirring occasionally. Serve in bowls topped with cheese, avocado, onion, tomatoes, and sour cream.

Yield: 8 servings

Contrary to popular belief, chili is not an authentic Mexican dish. To those in Mexico, chili means the pepper.

Chicken Fajitas

⅓	cup soy sauce		salt and pepper
½	cup lemon juice	12	flour tortillas
½	cup water		Toppings: Shredded lettuce,
1	tablespoon garlic powder		chopped tomatoes,
1	teaspoon ground cumin		grated cheese,
6	boneless, skinless chicken breasts		guacamole, and salsa.

Combine soy sauce and next four ingredients together in a heavy zip top bag. Tenderize chicken and sprinkle with salt and pepper. Place chicken in marinade and refrigerate about 3 hours. Grill chicken until no longer pink. Cut breasts into strips and serve wrapped in flour tortillas with all the toppings

Don't forget the rice and beans!

Yield: 12 servings

This marinade is terrific for beef, pork, or shrimp fajitas. Marinate shrimp for 3 hours. Marinate beef and pork for 24 hours.

Chicken Enchiladas Verde

6	boneless, skinless chicken breasts	1	(8-ounce) package cream cheese
2	onions, one quartered, one chopped	1	(8-ounce) carton sour cream
2	carrots, quartered	12-16	flour tortillas
½ -1	teaspoon salt	1½	cups grated Monterey Jack Cheese
¼	cup butter or margarine		
2	(4-ounce) cans chopped green chilies		

Topping

1	pint heavy cream	1½	cups red salsa, hot or mild
1½	cups green salsa, hot or mild		

The word salsa means sauce in Spanish, but is commonly used as a condiment.

Boil chicken in water with quartered onion, carrots, and salt. Remove chicken when done and reserve ½ cup broth. Cool chicken and shred. Sauté chopped onion in butter until soft. Add chilies, cream cheese and sour cream. Heat, but do not boil. Remove from heat and add chicken. Fill each tortilla with chicken mixture; roll, and place seam side down in 3-quart baking dish. Sprinkle with cheese. In a medium bowl combine reserved broth, cream, and both salsas. Pour over enchiladas and bake at 350° for 45 minutes.

This can be prepared in advance and frozen before adding broth and salsa mixture.

Yield: 6 servings

Pollo con Cilantro

Cilantro is the leaf of the coriander plant. It has a very clean, distinctive flavor. The seed has a very different flavor and is ground before use.

1	small onion, chopped	¼	teaspoon pepper
1	clove garlic, minced	3	tablespoons chopped cilantro
2	tablespoons margarine	½	cup chicken broth
4	boneless, skinless chicken breasts, cut in 1-inch pieces	2	cups rice cooked in chicken broth
1	teaspoon salt		

Sauté onion and garlic in margarine until soft. Add chicken, salt, and pepper and cook over medium heat until chicken is done. Stir in cilantro and broth, scraping bits from bottom of pan. Bring to a boil and cook for 2 minutes. Serve over rice and top with pan juices.

Yield: 4 servings

¡VIVA! Tradiciones

Chicken and Rice Picante

6	boneless, skinless chicken breasts	1	cup medium salsa or picante sauce
salt to taste		1	cup converted rice
¾	cup coarsely chopped onion	1	avocado, peeled and sliced
3	large garlic cloves, minced	1	medium tomato, chopped
1	tablespoon vegetable oil	½	cup grated Cheddar cheese
1¼	cups chicken broth		

Season chicken breasts with salt; set aside. In a 10-inch skillet, sauté onion and garlic in oil until soft. Add chicken broth and salsa, bring to a boil, and stir in rice. Arrange chicken breasts over rice. Cover tightly and simmer 20 minutes. Remove from heat, top with cheese, and let stand five minutes. Garnish with avocado and tomato.

Easy one dish meal.

Yield: 6 servings

Food hot from the fire is referred to as caliente, while spicy-hot is picante.

Bowtie Chicken and Spinach

1	(12-ounce) package bowtie pasta (farfalle)	2	cloves garlic, minced
2	tablespoons olive oil	3	Roma tomatoes, chopped
2	boneless, skinless chicken breasts, cubed	3	tablespoons lemon juice
1	(10-ounce) package frozen chopped spinach, thawed and drained	1	teaspoon seasoned salt
		½	teaspoon pepper
		1	cup grated Mozzarella cheese

Cook pasta according to package directions and drain. Place cooked pasta, lemon juice, and tomatoes in a large bowl. Set aside. Sauté chicken and garlic in oil for 3 minutes. Add spinach and cook for 5 minutes, stirring gently. Add chicken/spinach to pasta and toss gently. Season with salt and pepper, sprinkle with cheese, toss again.

Yield: 4 servings

Chicken Breasts Stuffed with Dried Tomatoes and Basil

¼	cup chopped fresh basil	1	teaspoon coarsely ground black pepper, divided
¼	cup chopped sundried tomatoes, drain and reserve oil		
2	tablespoons Parmesan cheese	4	boneless chicken breasts, with skin
		¼	teaspoon salt

In a small bowl, mix basil, dried tomatoes, Parmesan cheese, and ½ teaspoon pepper. Carefully push fingers between skin and meat of chicken breasts to form a pocket. Place 1 tablespoon basil mixture in each pocket. Place breasts in baking dish; brush with reserved oil. Sprinkle with salt and remaining pepper. Bake at 425° for 30 minutes. Garnish with whole basil leaves.

Serve with steamed red potatoes and broccoli.

Yield: 4 servings

Pat Magee's Surf Shop in Port Aransas lays claim to the only Surf Museum in Texas. It also is one of the biggest and best surf museums in the world. Drop in for a visit!

Chicken in Mustard Cream Sauce

4	boneless, skinless chicken breasts	¼	cup whipping cream
⅛	teaspoon pepper	¼	cup dry white wine
1	tablespoon Dijon mustard	2	teaspoons Dijon mustard
2	tablespoons olive oil	1	teaspoon green peppercorns, drained

Flatten chicken breasts to ¼-inch thick between 2 sheets of plastic wrap. Sprinkle with pepper and spread one side with mustard. Cook chicken in oil over medium heat for 10 minutes, turning once. Remove and keep warm. Combine remaining ingredients in skillet and simmer until mixture thickens, spoon over chicken breasts and serve.

Yield: 4 servings

Tessy's Chicken Curry

¼ cup butter or margarine	½ cup milk
1 small onion, chopped	cooked rice
⅓ cup flour	Condiments: chopped nuts,
⅛ teaspoon pepper	chopped onion,
2 teaspoons curry powder	pineapple tidbits,
½ teaspoon Worcestershire	shredded coconut, grated
sauce	ginger, chopped olives,
2 cups chicken broth	raisins, chutney
2½ cups cooked, diced	
chicken	

Sauté onion in butter until soft. Stir in flour and next three ingredients. Add broth and cook until thick, stirring constantly. Add chicken and milk. Heat thoroughly. Serve over hot rice with a selection of condiments.

Yield: 4 servings

Serve over saffron-flavored rice with a side dish of carrots sautéed in butter and brown sugar.

Bueno Pollo

¼ cup olive oil	1 tablespoon chopped
boneless, skinless	fresh parsley
chicken breasts	1 teaspoon pepper
(7-ounce) can whole	½ teaspoon salt
green chilies, cut into	½ cup grated Swiss cheese
½-inch strips	cooked rice
cup whipping cream	

Brown chicken in hot oil. Place chicken in a 2-quart glass baking dish. Arrange chilies over chicken. Whisk cream, parsley, pepper, and salt in a bowl and pour over chicken. Sprinkle with cheese and bake at 350° for 45 minutes, basting once or twice. Serve over rice.

Yield: 4 servings

Italian Chicken Roll-ups

1	(10-ounce) package frozen chopped broccoli	1	(8-ounce) can tomato sauce
½	onion, chopped	¼	teaspoon dried oregano
4	boneless, skinless chicken breasts, pounded flat	¼	teaspoon dried basil
		¼	teaspoon garlic powder
	salt and pepper	2	tablespoons Parmesan cheese
4	slices Mozzarella cheese		

This recipe uses homemade spaghetti sauce. If pressed for time, you can use your favorite store bought.

Cook broccoli and onion in ½ cup water for 7 minutes. Drain and divide in 4 portions. Season chicken breasts with salt and pepper. Lay a slice of cheese on each breast and top with broccoli. Roll up, secure with toothpick, and place rolls in baking dish. Combine tomato sauce and next 3 ingredients; pour over rolls. Sprinkle with cheese and bake at 350° for 45 minutes.

Yield: 4 servings

Chicken Pasta Parmesan

½	cup olive oil	6	tablespoons Parmesan cheese, divided
1	tablespoon dried oregano, crushed	6	chicken breasts
	salt and pepper to taste	¾	cup dry white wine
2	cloves garlic, minced	1	pound pasta, cooked and drained

This is not just any ordinary Chicken Parmesan dish!

Combine first 4 ingredients plus 3 tablespoons of Parmesan cheese; set aside. In large shallow baking dish, arrange chicken in single layer. Coat chicken with Parmesan cheese mixture and refrigerate covered for several hours. Bring to room temperature and redistribute marinade over chicken. Sprinkle with wine followed by remaining Parmesan cheese. Bake at 350° for 1 hour, basting occasionally. Remove from oven, transfer chicken to serving platter. Toss pasta in pan drippings. Serve chicken with pasta and additional Parmesan cheese.

Yield: 6 main course servings

Marinated Chicken Kabobs

½	cup lemon or lime juice	⅛	teaspoon black pepper
⅓	cup chutney	1	cup dry white wine
3	tablespoons vegetable oil	4-6	skinless, boneless
1	tablespoon red wine		chicken breasts, cubed
	vinegar	2	zucchini, cubed
1	clove garlic	1	yellow squash, cubed
1	teaspoon dry mustard	½	pound mushrooms,
½	teaspoon salt		halved
1	teaspoon red pepper	1	red bell pepper, cored,
	flakes		seeded, and cubed

Combine first 10 ingredients in blender until smooth. Place in zip top bag with chicken. Refrigerate 4 hours. Remove chicken and reserve marinade. Skewer chicken alternating vegetables and place kabobs in pan. Pour remaining marinade over skewers. Grill over hot coals 10 to 15 minutes, turning and basting occasionally with marinade.

Shrimp can be substituted for chicken.

Yield: 4 to 6 servings

Traditionally in Mexico, it is common practice to eat five meals a day. Early breakfast or desayuno, midmorning or almuerzo, dinner or comida, merienda, a late afternoon meal, and then late evening supper or cena.

Chicken with Artichokes

	boneless, skinless		salt and pepper
	chicken breasts	1	(6-ounce) jar marinated
¼	cup olive oil		artichokes with liquid
¼	pound mushrooms,	1	cup white wine
	sliced	¼	cup sliced black olives
¼	cup flour		

Brown chicken in oil; remove. In same pan, sauté mushrooms. Place chicken and mushrooms in a shallow 3-quart casserole. Add flour and seasonings to pan drippings and mix well. Coarsely chop artichokes and add with their liquid and wine, stir until smooth. Add olives and cook for 3 minutes. Pour artichoke sauce over chicken. Bake, covered, at 300° for 30 minutes.

Serve over rice garnished with chopped parsley or chives.

Yield: 4 servings

Waldorf Chicken

6	boneless, skinless chicken breasts	1	teaspoon ground ginger
1	cup unsweetened apple juice, divided	2	cups chopped red apples
		1	cup sliced celery
1	tablespoon cornstarch	¼	cup raisins
1	tablespoon lemon juice	1	sliced green onion with top
¼	teaspoon salt	½	cup chopped walnuts

Corpus Christi Harbor serves as the resting place for the Columbus Fleet. These ships are replicas built by Spain and given to our fair city as a gift. The Niña, Pinta, and Santa Maria are available for daily tours and can often be seen sailing the bay.

Place chicken, ½ cup apple juice, and next 3 ingredients in 10-inch non-stick skillet. Bring to boil and reduce heat. Cover and simmer until chicken is tender, about 20 minutes. Remove chicken and keep warm. Mix remaining apple juice with cornstarch, add to skillet. Bring to boil, stirring constantly, and reduce heat. Replace chicken and next 3 ingredients and simmer until sauce thickens. Stir in next 4 ingredients and heat through. Remove chicken and cut diagonally. Serve topped with sauce and sprinkled with walnuts.

Yield: 6 servings

Capered Lemon Chicken

2	tablespoons olive oil	1	teaspoon Italian herb seasoning
4	boneless, skinless chicken breasts	1	dash black pepper or cayenne
1	cup chopped onion	1-2	tablespoons small capers
4	cloves garlic, crushed	2	lemons, sliced very thin
1	cup sliced mushrooms	1	cup chopped fresh Italian parsley
2	cups dry white wine		

In large heavy skillet sauté chicken in oil until brown on both sides. Remove. In same skillet, sauté onion, garlic, and mushrooms for 3 minutes. Add wine, Italian seasoning, and pepper. Replace chicken and simmer for 3 minutes. Add capers, lemons, and parsley. Cover and simmer 6 to 8 minutes until chicken is tender.

Yield: 4 servings

Sesame Yogurt Chicken

1	cup bread crumbs	½	teaspoon pepper
¼	cup Parmesan cheese	8	ounces plain yogurt
1½	tablespoons minced onion	4	boneless, skinless chicken breasts
1	teaspoon garlic powder	2	tablespoons olive oil
¼	teaspoon oregano, dried	2	tablespoons sesame seeds
¼	teaspoon thyme, dried		
1	teaspoon salt		

In shallow dish mix together first 8 ingredients. Coat chicken with yogurt, and roll in bread crumb mixture. Place chicken in a lightly greased baking dish. Drizzle with olive oil and sprinkle with sesame seeds. Bake uncovered at 350° for 45 minutes.

Yield: 4 servings

Our neighbors to the north in Rockport-Fulton are host to the annual Hummer/Bird Celebration held in September. Bird-lovers flock to the area for this special event.

Chicken Betty B.

	2½ pound frying chicken, cut up	2½	teaspoons salt
3	tablespoons oil	¼	teaspoon pepper
	cup sliced onion	1	teaspoon tarragon
	clove garlic, minced	⅛	teaspoon thyme
¾	cups chicken broth	⅛	teaspoon marjoram
	cup wild rice blend, uncooked	1	(12-ounce) package frozen French-style green beans, thawed

In a deep heavy skillet, brown chicken in oil. Remove chicken. In same skillet lightly sauté onions and garlic. Add chicken broth, rice, and seasonings. Stir well. Lay chicken over rice and top with green beans; cover pan tightly. Cook over low heat 20 minutes, until rice is done.

Yield: 6 servings

Spinach Chicken Casserole

1	(4-5 pound) whole chicken	1	teaspoon pepper
1	(8-ounce) package egg noodles	1	teaspoon salt
¼	cup butter	1	(10-ounce package) spinach, cooked and drained
¼	cup flour		
1	cup half & half or whole milk	1	(6-ounce) can mushrooms with juice
2	cups sour cream	1	(8-ounce) can water chestnuts, chopped
⅓	cup lemon juice		
2	teaspoons seasoned salt	½	cup chopped onion
½	teaspoon cayenne pepper	½	cup chopped celery
		1	(4-ounce) can pimento
1	teaspoon paprika	1½	cups grated Monterey Jack cheese

Mexican fiestas are common to South Texas. On pleasant evenings, patios are lit with luminarios and mariachis serenade guests who are amply supplied with margaritas.

Boil chicken and reserve broth. Bone and cut in bite-size pieces. Reserve 1 cup broth and cook noodles in remaining broth; drain. In skillet, melt butter and stir in flour until smooth. Gradually stir in milk and 1 cup reserved broth, stir until smooth. Add sour cream and next 6 ingredients; mix well. Combine chicken, milk mixture, and cooked noodles in large bowl. Add spinach and next 5 ingredients, mix well. Pour into a 9x13 casserole and top with cheese. Bake at 350° for 45 minutes.

Freezes well.

Yield: 8 servings

Orange Chicken

2	pounds boneless, skinless chicken breasts	¼	cup chopped green onions
6	tablespoons butter, divided	2	tablespoons flour
		¾	cup chicken broth
½	cup sliced mushrooms	½	cup fresh orange juice

Sauté chicken in 4 tablespoons butter until brown on each side and remove. In same skillet sauté mushrooms and green onions until soft. In separate pan melt remaining 2 tablespoons butter and mix in flour to form paste. Add broth and orange juice, cook until thickened, stirring constantly. Place chicken in shallow casserole dish and top with mushrooms and sauce. Cover and bake at 375° for 25 to 30 minutes.

Yield: 6 servings

Turkey Parmesan

¼	cup butter	2	tablespoons dry white wine
½	cup chopped onion	2	teaspoons Worcestershire sauce
½	cup chopped celery	½	teaspoon salt
½	cup sliced mushrooms	½	teaspoon pepper
2	cloves garlic, minced	½	teaspoon poultry seasoning
½	cup all-purpose flour	5	drops Tabasco
4	cups milk	¼	teaspoon cayenne pepper
4	cups cubed cooked turkey	4	cups egg noodles, cooked
⅓	cup Parmesan cheese		
2	tablespoons chopped fresh parsley		

From kids to grandparents, everyone loves this dish. Make it with leftover turkey or chicken.

Melt butter in a large, heavy skillet. Sauté onion and next 3 ingredients until tender. Add flour, stirring until smooth. Gradually add milk and cook over medium heat, stirring constantly, until thick. Add remaining ingredients, except noodles, and stir until heated through. Serve over hot noodles.

Yield: 8 servings

Chicken Ratatouille

¼	cup oil	½	pound mushrooms, sliced
8	boneless, skinless chicken breasts, cubed	1	(16-ounce) can diced tomatoes
2	zucchini, sliced	1	clove garlic, minced
	eggplant, peeled and cubed	1	teaspoon basil
	large onion, sliced	1	tablespoon chopped parsley
	bell pepper, sliced		salt and pepper to taste

Sauté chicken in hot oil about 2 minutes each side. Add zucchini and next 4 ingredients. Cook 7 to 10 minutes. Add tomatoes and stir gently. Add garlic and seasonings; simmer for 5 minutes.

Yield: 4 servings

Curried Chicken Casserole

1	(3-pound) whole chicken	1	pound mushrooms, sliced
1	cup water		
1	cup sherry	2	tablespoons butter
2	tablespoons curry powder	1	cup sour cream
		1	(10¾-ounce) can cream of mushroom soup
1	cup diced celery		
1	onion, chopped	1	(14-ounce) can artichoke hearts, chopped and drained
¼	teaspoon salt		
¼	teaspoon pepper		
1½	cups wild rice blend	½	cup slivered almonds

Combine chicken and next 7 ingredients in a large stock pot. Cover and cook one hour. Remove and bone chicken, reserving broth. Skim fat from broth and add water to make 2½ cups broth. Cook rice in broth, covered, for 20 minutes. Cut chicken into bite-size pieces. While rice is cooking, sauté mushrooms in butter until tender. Stir in chicken, sour cream, soup, and artichokes. Combine chicken mixture with rice. Place in 3-quart casserole, sprinkle with almonds, cover, and bake at 350° for 45 minutes.

Chicken breasts can be substituted for whole chicken.

Yield: 8 servings

Chicken Tetrazzini

1	(4-5 pound) whole chicken	1	(8-ounce) package spaghetti, broken into thirds
4	tablespoons onion, diced		
4	tablespoons butter	1	(10¾-ounce) can cream of chicken soup
1	(4-ounce) can sliced mushrooms		
		1	(12-ounce) can evaporated milk
1	(2-ounce) jar diced pimento		
		½	cup Parmesan cheese
⅛	teaspoon cayenne pepper	1	cup grated Velveeta
		1	cup grated Cheddar cheese
½	teaspoon marjoram		

Boil chicken, reserving broth. Bone, and cut in bite-size pieces. Sauté onion until tender. Add mushrooms and next 3 ingredients; simmer 2 minutes. Boil spaghetti in broth al dente. Drain. Combine all ingredients, except cheeses, and pour in greased 3-quart baking dish. Sprinkle with cheeses and bake at 350° for 30 to 40 minutes.

Freezes well.

Yield: 6 to 8 servings

Meat

Ranching

A century ago, wild horses, longhorn cattle, javalina, fox, and deer roamed the lands of South Texas. They were descendants of the animals left by Spanish explorers and earlier pioneers of the area. More were left after Texas won its independence from Mexico in 1936, marking the Rio Grande River as the border between the Republic of Texas and Mexico. Some Mexican ranchers north of the Rio Grande abandoned their herds to move south, within their nation's new border. Taking lessons from the Spanish methods of working cattle, Texans took control of livestock herds on horseback, which they had not done before. Soon, the ranching industry in which Texas would become known for, was born. Many large South Texas ranches were established in the 1800's. None is better known than the King Ranch, founded in 1853 by Richard King and recognized as the birth place of the American ranching industry. Headquartered in Kingsville, forty-five miles south of Corpus Christi, it claims the development of the Santa Gertrudis, and King Ranch Santa Cruz cattle breed, and was responsible for producing the first registered American Quarter Horse. King Ranch covers more land than the entire state of Rhode Island — 825,000 acres and is home to over 60,000 cattle and 300 Quarter Horses. Of course, ranching is a tradition also enjoyed on a much smaller scale, perhaps on a few hundred or a few thousand acres, by many South Texans. More are residents who work in the area cities during the week and make ranching a weekend sideline. Some make their living on the land by raising cattle or crops. Whatever their purpose, many South Texas ranches are places where some of the areas native wildlife can thrive, or at least survive. Ranches and national wildlife refuges are safe havens for many of the areas native animals, such as javalina, wild turkey and deer. King Ranch and Kennedy Ranch, as well as state parks and nationally known preserves such as Aransas National Wildlife Refuge and Wilder Wildlife Refuge, offer a glimpse of the areas many animal species, reptiles, amphibians, and birding life that have roamed this area for centuries.

¡VIVA! Tradiciones

¡VIVA! Tournedos

1	teaspoon salt	1	cup chopped onion
1/4	teaspoon garlic powder	1	cup diced tomatoes
1/4	teaspoon black pepper	8	ounces mushrooms,
1/2	teaspoon paprika		sliced
4	filet mignons	1	clove garlic, minced
3	tablespoons butter,	2	teaspoons black pepper
	divided		

Combine first 4 ingredients and sprinkle on meat. Over medium heat, melt 3 tablespoons butter. Sauté steaks to desired degree of doneness, about 3 minutes per side for medium-rare. Remove filets and keep warm. In the same pan, sauté onion and next 3 ingredients until onions are soft, about 3 minutes. Stir in remaining butter and pepper. Remove from heat and spoon sauce over steaks.

Yield: 4 servings

The King Ranch is the largest working ranch in the United States with 825,000 acres. It was founded by Captain Richard King in 1867.

Herb-coated Tenderloin

1	cup flour	4	tablespoons seasoned
2	tablespoons chopped		salt
	fresh rosemary	4	tablespoons seasoned
2	tablespoons dry mustard		pepper
		1	(3-pound) beef tenderloin

Mix first 5 ingredients well. Store in jar until ready to use. Preheat oven to 500°. Pat tenderloin generously with coating. Place in a greased roasting pan. Roast for 25 to 30 minutes or until meat thermometer reaches 140° for medium-rare. Slice in 1/2-inch medallions.

Store leftover coating mix in a sealed jar.

Yield: 8 servings

This herb mixture also suits venison backstrap.

Tenderloins with Mustard Sauce

4	(4-ounce) tenderloin steaks	¼	cup brandy
3	tablespoons coarse black pepper	1	tablespoon Dijon mustard
2	shallots, minced	⅓	cup whipping cream
		salt	

Coat steaks with pepper. Sear steaks in heavy greased skillet, about 2 minutes per side. Transfer to roasting pan and bake at 350° for 8 minutes, for medium-rare. In same skillet, sauté shallots until soft, add brandy, and cook for 1 minute, stirring constantly. Stir in mustard and cream. Simmer for 2 minutes and serve with steaks.

Yield: 4 servings

Dijon mustard comes from the ancient French province of Burgundy.

Mexican Mushroom Steak

Meat

6	rib-eye steaks	1	tablespoon ground cumin
⅓	cup soy sauce	1	teaspoon chili powder
2	tablespoons minced garlic	1	teaspoon fresh ground pepper

Mushroom Salsa

2	tablespoons oil	½	cup chopped pecans
1	pound mushrooms, stemmed and quartered	2	tablespoons red wine vinegar
1	teaspoon dried rosemary	½	teaspoon garlic powder
1	red bell pepper, diced	salt and pepper	
3	green onions, chopped		

Marinate steaks in soy sauce 1 hour. Combine garlic and next 3 ingredients. Remove steaks from soy sauce and rub with garlic mixture. Grill or sauté to desired degree of doneness. For sauce: sauté mushrooms in oil until soft. Add rosemary and remove from heat. Place remaining ingredients in a bowl. Add mushrooms and toss. Serve at room temperature with steaks.

Yield: 6 servings

To test salsa, drop some on the tablecloth ... if it fails to burn a hole in the cloth, it is not a good sauce! (Just for laughs guys!!!)

¡VIVA! Tradiciones

Blue Cheese Steaks

½ cup butter	dash of red pepper
4 ounces blue cheese	4 rib-eye steaks, room
3-4 cloves garlic, minced	temperature
2 tablespoons dried	coarse black pepper
parsley	

Combine first 5 ingredients in saucepan over medium heat until smooth and paste like; do not boil. Remove from heat. Season steaks with coarse black pepper. Grill one side over hot coals, flip and spread cooked side with blue cheese mixture. Continue to grill until desired degree of doneness. Remove steaks and spread cheese on other side. Serve immediately with remaining spread.

This spread also is scrumptious with bread. Coat each slice and broil until cheese bubbles.

Yield: 4 servings

Any good quality steak will give delicious results.

Sour Cream Roast

1 (3-4 pound) boneless roast	1 onion, sliced in rings
2 tablespoons oil	¾ cup dry red wine
1 teaspoon salt	1 cup sour cream
1 teaspoon pepper	2 tablespoons flour
1 clove garlic, minced	1½ cups water
1 large carrot, sliced	juice of ½ lemon

Pat meat dry and season with salt and pepper. In Dutch oven, brown all sides; remove roast. In same pan, sauté garlic, carrots and onions for 3 minutes. Return roast to pan. Add wine and coat roast with sour cream. Cover and bake at 300° for 2 hours. Remove meat from pan. Add flour mixed with water to pan drippings and cook 3 to 5 minutes over medium heat, stirring constantly. Add lemon juice and pour sauce over sliced roast.

Yield: 6 to 8 servings

A South Texas treat, wrapped in a flour tortilla.

Flank Steak Extraordinaire

½ cup soy sauce
2 tablespoons Worcestershire sauce
1 tablespoon lemon juice
2 tablespoons brown sugar
1 clove garlic, chopped
½ teaspoon powdered ginger
1½ pounds flank steak

Mix first 6 ingredients in small saucepan over medium heat until sugar melts. Pour over meat and marinate several hours. Remove meat and reserve marinade. Grill meat over hot coals for 5 to 10 minutes each side. Slice against grain and serve with reserved marinade that has been boiled for 1 minute.

Yield: 4 servings

Burgundy Beef Tenderloin

1¾ pounds beef tenderloin
1½ cups safflower oil
¾ cup soy sauce
¼ cup Worcestershire sauce
2 tablespoons dry mustard
½ cup lemon juice
½ cup red wine vinegar
4 cloves garlic, minced
¼ cup chopped parsley

Pat meat dry and place in a roasting pan. Combine all remaining ingredients and pour over meat. Bake at 350° for 45 minutes, basting occasionally.

Yield: 4 servings

Avocado Steak

2 pounds, cooked tenderloin, sliced thin
2 avocados, diced
1 red onion, sliced thin
½ cup oil
¼ cup olive oil
½ cup wine vinegar
2 teaspoons Dijon mustard
2 teaspoons salt
¼ teaspoon pepper
⅓ bunch parsley, chopped

A refreshing cold dish.

Layer strips of meat in bottom of large casserole. Top with avocado and onions. Repeat layers. Combine oil with remaining ingredients and pour over meat. Marinate overnight. Serve with a slotted spoon.

Yield: 6 servings

¡VIVA! Tradiciones

So-simple Soft Tacos

2	pounds ground beef	2	(8-ounce) cans tomato sauce
1	onion, chopped		
3	tablespoons chopped jalapeños	2	cups grated sharp Cheddar cheese
4	cloves garlic, crushed	20	corn tortillas
1	teaspoon ground pepper		shredded lettuce
½	teaspoon cayenne pepper		chopped tomatoes
1	tablespoon fajita seasoning		sour cream
			salsa

Brown beef with onion, jalapeños, and garlic. Drain grease. Add remaining seasonings and tomato sauce; heat through. Remove from heat and top with cheese. Soften tortillas in oil or sprinkle with water and microwave for 30 seconds. Place meat mixture in tortillas and top with lettuce, tomato, salsa, and sour cream.

Do not use fajita marinade.

Yield: 6 to 8 servings

Corn tortillas are exceptionally low in fat, high in complex carbohydrates, and have no cholesterol.

Sour Cream Beef Enchiladas

1	pound ground beef	16	corn tortillas
½	cup chopped onion	¼	cup margarine
2	cloves garlic, minced	1	tablespoon flour
1	teaspoon chili powder	2	cups chicken broth
	salt and pepper	1	cup chopped green chilies
½	cups grated sharp Cheddar cheese	1-1½	cups sour cream

Brown meat with onions and garlic. Season with chili powder, salt and pepper. Sprinkle a small amount of water between tortillas, wrap in paper towel, and microwave 30 seconds to soften. Fill each tortilla with meat and sprinkle of cheese. Roll and place seam side down in 9x13 baking dish. May freeze at this point. In a medium saucepan melt butter and stir in flour. While stirring, slowly add broth and continue to cook until thickened. Remove from heat and add chilies and sour cream. Pour sauce over enchiladas. Bake at 375° for 25 minutes.

Yield: 8 servings

Longhorn cattle are descendants of cattle left in Texas by Spanish explorers before the mid-18th century. These cattle helped save the state from post Civil War economic collapse.

155

Meats

Fideo con Carne

1	pound ground meat
½	cup chopped onion
½	cup chopped bell pepper
1	tablespoon taco seasoning
1	clove garlic, minced
1	tablespoon vegetable oil

1	(5-ounce) box Vermicelli
1	(15-ounce) can beef broth
1	teaspoon cumin
1	teaspoon black pepper
1	(14½-ounce) can diced tomatoes

Brown meat with onion and next 3 ingredients. Drain grease and set meat aside. Heat oil in skillet and sauté vermicelli until lightly brown. Add meat and remaining ingredients, stir well. Cover and simmer 15 minutes.

Replace meat with pinto beans for a spicy meatless entrée.

Yield: 4 servings

Mexican Lasagne

1	pound ground beef
1	onion, chopped
1	bell pepper, chopped
2	cloves garlic, minced
1	teaspoon salt
¼	teaspoon black pepper
2	tablespoons chili powder
1	(10-ounce) can diced tomatoes with green chilies
1	(8-ounce) can tomato sauce

1	cup water
1	(14-ounce) can pinto beans, drained
1	cup sour cream
1	cup cottage cheese
10 to 14 flour tortillas
1	cup grated Monterey Jack cheese
Toppings: chopped tomatoes, green onion, black olives and avocado

Easy company dish, one serving will not be enough!

Brown meat with onion and next 5 ingredients. Drain off grease. Add tomatoes, tomato sauce, and water. Simmer 5 minutes over medium heat. Add beans and stir. Process sour cream and cottage cheese in blender until smooth. Cut each tortilla into long strips. Place a small amount of meat mixture in bottom of greased 9x13 casserole. Layer half of tortilla strips over meat mixture. Layer half of remaining meat mixture and top with all the sour cream. Sprinkle with half of the cheese. Place another layer of tortilla strips and cover with remaining meat mixture, top with last of cheese. Bake at 350° for 20 minutes.

May substitute corn tortillas.

Yield: 6 servings

¡VIVA! Tradiciones

Sensational Sesame Pork

3	pounds boneless pork loin	2	cloves garlic, finely minced
1	cup soy sauce	2	teaspoons ground ginger
3	tablespoons brown sugar	2	tablespoons oil
3	tablespoons finely minced onion	½	cup plus 2 tablespoons sesame seeds, divided

Place meat in deep pan. Combine the next 6 ingredients with ½ cup sesame seeds. Pour over meat and refrigerate at least 3 hours, turning meat often. Insert meat thermometer into thickest part and sprinkle with remaining 2 tablespoons sesame seeds. Bake with marinade at 400° for 10 minutes. Baste and lower heat to 325°. Cook for 1½ hours, or until thermometer reaches 155°. Drain off sauce and slice in thin medallions.

Serve with fresh pineapple and seasoned rice. Great marinade for thick pork chops.

Yield: 6 to 8 servings

Tamales, a South Texas holiday tradition, are in such demand at Christmas time that you must place your order with your favorite tamale maker weeks in advance.

Grilled Pork Tenderloin

½	cup soy sauce	2	tablespoons brown sugar
½	cup sherry	1	teaspoon dry mustard
3	cloves garlic, minced	6	green onions, chopped
½	teaspoon pepper	2	pounds pork tenderloin
1	inch square grated fresh ginger		

Combine soy sauce with next 7 ingredients. Place tenderloin in large zip top plastic bag and pour in marinade. Refrigerate 12 to 24 hours. Remove meat and reserve marinade. Grill over hot coals, 8 minutes per side. Bring reserved marinade to boil for 1 minute and serve with meat.

Southern treat served with sweet potatoes.

Yield: 4 to 6 servings

Crown Roast of Pork

A exquisite crown roast filled with savory stuffing … perfect for any special occasion.

Meat

1	crown roast of pork, cut from loin and tied together
1	clove garlic

freshly ground pepper
flour

1	cup apple cider

Dressing

2	tablespoons butter
1	medium onion, chopped
1	clove garlic, minced
2	cups tart apples, cored and diced
4	cups cooked wild rice blend
⅓	cup toasted pine nuts or pecans
¼	cup raisins, plumped in a little cider

¼	cup finely diced ham
2	tablespoons chopped fresh parsley
½	teaspoon dried sage
½	teaspoon dried thyme
1	teaspoon coriander
½	cup chopped celery
¼	teaspoon nutmeg
⅛	teaspoon ground cumin

salt and pepper
paper crowns

Have a butcher prepare and tie crown roast in a ring using 1 or 2 pieces of loin, allowing 2 chops per person. Scrape ends of rib bones down to lean meat. Cover exposed bones with foil to prevent scorching. Rub meat with cut clove of garlic and sprinkle with pepper. Dust any fat with a little flour to make it crispy. Pour cider in large baking pan, add roast, and bake at 325° for 30 minutes per pound, or until internal temperature has reached 180°. Baste meat, often with pan juices. While roast is baking, prepare stuffing. Sauté onion and garlic in butter until soft. Add apples and sauté for 5 minutes. Add cooked rice and remaining ingredients. Spoon stuffing in middle of crown 30 to 40 minutes before roast is done; finish cooking roast. Remove from oven and place paper crowns on rib bones and surroun with your favorite steamed vegetables.

A meat thermometer will ensure the roast is not overcooked.

Yield: Allow 2 chops per person

Indonesian Pork Roast

1	(5-6 pound) pork shoulder roast	1	cup boiling water
2	cloves garlic, minced	¼	cup brown sugar
1	chicken bouillon cube	½	cup soy sauce

Brown pork in its own fat in a large heavy Dutch oven or covered pot. Dissolve bouillon in boiling water. Combine with remaining ingredients and pour over meat. Cover and simmer on top of stove over low heat, for 2 to 2½ hours, turning meat twice.

For extra flavor, add dry mustard and chopped onion to gravy. Serve over rice.

Yield: 8 servings

The most tender, savory roast you will ever eat.

Alsatian Pork Roast

Rub

1	cup salt	1	teaspoon garlic powder
½	cup white pepper	1	teaspoon onion powder
1	tablespoon paprika	1	teaspoon allspice

Roast

1	(3-pound) pork roast	1½	cups heavy cream
3	slices bacon, diced	1	tablespoon tarragon mustard
2	cups sliced mushrooms		
1	large carrot, sliced	½	cup small capers, drained
1	stalk celery, sliced	1	tablespoon horseradish
2¼	cups white wine	1	cup basic white sauce

Preheat oven to 400°. Combine all rub ingredients in a jar. Rub roast with spice mixture; reserve leftover rub. Lay bacon, mushrooms, carrot, and celery in bottom of Dutch oven. Place roast over vegetables. Bake for 15 minutes. Pour ½ of wine over and reduce heat to 375°, continue to bake 40 to 50 minutes. Remove roast from pan and keep warm. Place Dutch oven on stove top, over medium heat; add remaining wine and all remaining ingredients. Simmer while stirring until thick. Season with salt and pepper if needed. Slice roast and serve with sauce and vegetables.

Splendid the next day served cold.

Yield: 4 to 6 servings

Graciously submitted by Chef Bruno and his wife Fredrika from their gourmet restaurant, "Windows on the Bay".

Bourbon Pork Tenders

½	cup lite soy sauce	3	(¾ pound) pork
½	cup bourbon		tenderloin
4	tablespoons brown sugar		

Combine first 3 ingredients in shallow baking dish or plastic bag. Add meat and marinate overnight or for several hours. Grill over hot coals for 20 minutes, turning once. Baste occasionally with marinade.

Perfect for parties served sliced on rolls. May also bake at 325° for 45 minutes.

Yield: 6 to 8 servings

Pork Chops with Caper Sauce

4-6	pork chops	4	tablespoons capers,
salt and pepper			drained
1	tablespoon oil	1	tablespoon Dijon
½	cup finely chopped onion		mustard
2	cloves garlic, minced	3	tablespoons tomato
2	teaspoons red wine		sauce
	vinegar	1	teaspoon cornstarch
1	cup chicken broth		

Season pork chops with salt and pepper. In large skillet, over medium heat, sauté chops in oil. Remove and keep warm. Pour off excess oil and sauté onions and garlic in same skillet until soft. Add vinegar and next 4 ingredients. Cook until reduced by half. Dissolve cornstarch in 1 tablespoon water and add to sauce. Stir until thick. Remove from heat and season with salt and pepper. Pour sauce over warm chops and serve.

A side dish of spinach fettuccine or wild rice would be perfect with this divine entrée.

Yield: 4 to 6 servings

Hawaiian Baked Pork Chops

1   (20-ounce) can of
    crushed pineapple
3   medium sweet potatoes,
    peeled and sliced ½-inch
    thick

2   tablespoons brown sugar
4   pork chops
salt and pepper
2   tablespoons butter, cut in
    4 pieces

Place pineapple with juice in bottom of large baking dish. Place potatoes around and sprinkle with brown sugar. Season chops with salt and pepper. Brown slightly in a hot oiled skillet. Place chops over potatoes and dot each chop with butter. Cover and bake at 350° for 1 hour, or until potatoes are tender. Uncover and raise heat to 425°; cook for 10 minutes.

Yield: 4 servings

Burgundy Pork Chops

4   (1½-inch) butterflied
    boneless pork loin chops
Creole seasoning
½   cup butter
3   cloves garlic, minced
½   cup flour
1   tablespoon lemon pepper

2   (14-ounce) cans beef
    broth
½   cup Burgundy wine
1   tablespoon chopped
    parsley
2   cups sliced mushrooms
cooked rice

Season pork chops with Creole seasoning. Place in baking dish and bake at 325° for 30 to 40 minutes. While meat is cooking, sauté garlic in butter. Mix in flour and lemon pepper, stirring constantly, until medium brown. Gradually add broth and next 3 ingredients; stir until thick. Add mushrooms and cook 10 to 15 additional minutes. Slice pork and place over rice. Pour sauce over pork and rice.

Garnish with fresh parsley.

Yield: 6 to 8 servings

¡Bravo! Brisket

1	(7-9 pound) brisket salt and pepper	6	cloves garlic, whole
¼	cup Worcestershire sauce	¼	cup soy sauce
		¼	cup Louisiana style hot sauce
¼	cup bottled green jalapeño sauce	2	tablespoon ketchup
1	large onion, cubed	¼	cup lemon juice
4	cloves garlic, minced	2	tablespoons cornstarch

A talented pitperson can turn a tough hunk of brisket into a tender masterpiece. Many hours of philosophizing, beer drinking, and meat turning are shared in the backyards of people all across Texas.

Place brisket, fat side down, on a large sheet of heavy duty foil. Rub salt and pepper over brisket. Pour Worcestershire and green sauce over meat. Top with garlic and onion. Wrap securely in foil and grill over medium coals for 3 to 4 hours. Remove brisket from foil, reserving juices in bowl. Skim excess grease, leaving 1 cup of juice. Heat juice in saucepan with soy sauce, hot sauce, and ketchup. Dissolve cornstarch in lemon juice and add to sauce. Bring sauce to boil and cook until slightly thick. Pour over sliced brisket or serve on the side.

Yield: 6 to 8 servings

Believe It-or-not Brisket

1	(3½ pound) beef brisket	1	stick cinnamon
1	(12-ounce) can Coca-Cola	2	cloves, whole
2	cups barbecue sauce	4	peppercorns, whole

The Coca-Cola breaks down meat fibers, tenderizing the meat.

Cut fat from meat and place in glass baking dish or large zip top plastic bag. Pour cola over meat and seal. Refrigerate at least 8 hours, turning once. Preheat grill. Remove meat from cola. Place on 24x18-inch piece heavy duty foil. Pour barbecue sauce over meat. Add other ingredients and seal in foil. Cook over medium coals 2 to 3 hours. Slice and serve with sauce.

May bake in oven at 325° for 3 hours.

Yield: 6 to 8 servings

¡VIVA! Tradiciones

Veal Piccata with Capers

6-8 veal scollops, pounded
    thin
flour
salt and white pepper
1 tablespoon thyme
2 eggs, beaten

4 tablespoons olive oil
1 cup dry white wine
1 (3-ounce) jar capers,
    drained
juice of 1 lemon

Combine flour, salt, pepper, and thyme in bowl. Dip veal in egg and then in flour mixture. Sauté veal in olive oil until golden brown, remove, and keep warm. Deglaze pan with wine and lemon juice; reduce by ⅓. Add capers and stir gently until warm. Pour over veal and serve.

Yield: 4 servings

Peppercorn Lamb Chops

2 racks of lamb or chops,
    approximately
    2½-pounds
2 tablespoons olive oil
2 tablespoons chopped
    fresh rosemary
2 cloves garlic, chopped
salt and cracked black pepper
2 tablespoons butter

⅓ cup minced shallots
2 teaspoons cracked black
    pepper
½ cup white wine
2 cups beef broth
2 teaspoons tomato paste
1 tablespoon cornstarch,
    dissolved in ¼ cup water

Preheat oven to 500°. Rub lamb with oil. Season with rosemary, garlic, and pepper. Place lamb in baking pan, fat side up and roast for 10 minutes. Reduce oven temperature to 400° and continue to roast for 10 minutes. Meat should be medium rare at this point. Transfer to a plate and keep warm. In a skillet, sauté shallots in butter for 1 minute. Add 2 teaspoons peppercorns and wine, reduce by half. Add broth and tomato paste, bring to a boil, and reduce by half. Add dissolved cornstarch and stir over medium heat until thick. Pour sauce over warm chops and serve immediately.

Yield: 6 servings

Herbs love to be picked. They grow bushier and the "pruning" will lengthen your growing season.

A pepper plant in the yard brings good luck.

Garlic-crusted Leg of Lamb with Mint Salsa

Lamb

4-5 pounds leg of lamb, deboned and butterflied	4 cloves garlic, minced
salt and pepper	½ cup seasoned bread crumbs
olive oil	

Mint Salsa

3 cloves garlic, minced	½ cup diced onions
2 jalapeños, seed 1 and chop both	¼ cup lime juice
½ cup chopped fresh mint	¼ teaspoon salt
1 cup diced tomatoes	¼ teaspoon pepper

Trim fat from leg and score all sides. Season with salt and pepper and rub meat with oil. Mix garlic and bread crumbs and press mixture all over meat, forming a crust. Bake at 450° for 20 minutes or grill over hot coals with meat thermometer until temperature reaches 160°, for medium to medium rare. For salsa: mix all ingredients and refrigerate 2 or more hours. Slice meat and serve with cold salsa on side.

Yield: 8 to 10 servings

Hazelnut Leg of Lamb

1 leg of lamb	1 cup fine bread crumbs
salt and pepper	1 cup chopped hazelnuts
2 cloves garlic	½ teaspoon black pepper
1 tablespoon chopped fresh rosemary	⅓ cup butter

Trim fat from leg and season with salt and pepper. Blend remaining ingredients in food processor until fine. Place lamb in foil-lined roasting pan. Crust lamb with nut mixture. Roast at 350° for 2 hours. Lamb should be pink in the middle. Slice and serve.

Yield: 8 to 10 servings

Game

Wild Game and Fishing

From brush country to bay waters, South Texas' variety of natural habitats makes its home to a similarly wide assortment of wild game, from dove to deer to a 350-pound tarpon. For many South Texans hunting and fishing are a way of life. When hunting is mentioned it is likely to mean tracking whitetailed deer — the big bucks with sprawling antlers that make good trophies and stock the freezer with venison. During the winter migration, the region also becomes home to millions of dove and quail, as they pass through South Texas feeding on sunflowers and croton. The area also boasts javalina, geese, and wild turkey. A good hunting season is usually the result of average or better rainfall. When drought lessens the force of game in the brush country, South Texans can always turn to the coast to hunt waterfowl, such as teal, or to fish the Aransas Bay System. The four bays offer a range of distinctive fishing from shallow shorelines and lakes to oyster reefs and wells, including the grass flats. The shoreline of Corpus Christi Bay, one of the largest, has popular fishing spots both inside the city as well as farther north. Nueces Bay, or "Back Bay" has a number of reefs that attract fish and fishermen. Better known, though, are the waters of the upper Laguna Madre and especially Baffin Bay. Anyone looking to hook a trophy-size speckled trout should look here. In the city originally known as Tarpon, Port Aransas has become famous to many anglers in search of sharks, jack crevalle, and large stingrays. "Port A" as it is now referred to, is a harbor for fishing boats that make regular runs into the Gulf of Mexico for kingfish, ling, dolphin, amberjack, red snapper, bonito, and other species.

¡VIVA! Tradiciones

Cartwright's Roast Leg of Venison

1	leg of venison	2	tablespoons whole
2	pounds sliced bacon		comino
2	garlic pods, peeled	⅓	cup parsley
⅓	cup rosemary		salt and pepper to taste

Lay leg on foil-lined pan and cut slits all over. Cut half of bacon into thirds. Insert whole cloves of garlic and bacon pieces in each hole. Rub with spices and salt and pepper heavily. Drape remaining slices of bacon over top of venison. Roast uncovered at 325° allowing 30 minutes per pound.

The underbrush and scrubby trees that grow on South Texas ranchlands provide homes for a great variety of game including deer, dove, and quail.

Stuffed Venison Burgers

1	pound ground venison sausage	1	teaspoon pepper
1	pound ground beef	8	slices American cheese
3	tablespoons Worcestershire sauce	8	slices Swiss cheese
2	tablespoons steak sauce	1	medium onion, sliced
2	teaspoons seasoned salt	1	(7-ounce) can sliced jalapeño

Combine venison sausage, beef, Worcestershire, steak sauce, salt, and pepper. Form 16 thin patties. Lay a slice of American cheese over 8 patties. Top cheese with onion slice and a few jalapeño slices. Place a slice of Swiss cheese over jalapeño and top with remaining patty. Pinch edges to seal. Grill over hot coals or cook in skillet. Serve plain or make into burgers with all the fixings.

Yield: 8 burgers

Roast Venison with Hunter Sauce

1	leg of venison	1	medium onion, sliced
4	cloves garlic, slivered	5	tablespoons dried
1½	cups olive oil, divided		rosemary
4	cups red Burgundy wine	2	tablespoons freshly
1	cup Worcestershire sauce		ground black pepper

Pat meat dry and make deep incisions onto meat; insert garlic. Combine 1 cup oil and next 5 ingredients; pour over leg. Cover and refrigerate at least 12 hours, turning every few hours. Place in deep pan with half of the marinade. Pour remaining ½ cup olive oil over meat and bake uncovered at 450° for 15 minutes. Reduce heat to 250° and insert a meat thermometer in thickest part, without touching the bone. Cover with foil and bake, basting often, until thermometer reads 150° for medium (about 3 hours). Slice and serve with hunter sauce.

The secret to venison is to not over cook it. It is best when served medium rare to medium.

Hunter Sauce

2	tablespoons unsalted butter	1	cup fresh chopped tomatoes, peeled and seeded
2	tablespoons chopped green onions	1	teaspoon cornstarch
4	cups sliced mushrooms	1	teaspoon water
⅔	cup dry white wine	½	teaspoon freshly ground black pepper
1	cup deglazed pan drippings		salt to taste

In a large saucepan, melt butter over medium heat. Sauté green onions and mushrooms until tender. Add wine and simmer briefly. Add pan drippings and tomatoes; cook about 5 minutes. Tomatoes should be slightly firm. Dissolve cornstarch in water and stir into sauce; simmer until thick. Season with salt and pepper. Serve hot over venison.

Yield: 3 to 4 cups

Venison Jerky

3	pounds any venison parts, cut in thin strips	2	tablespoons chopped garlic
2	(4-ounce) bottles liquid smoke	2	teaspoons salt
¼	cup steak sauce	1	teaspoon onion salt
2	tablespoons Worcestershire sauce	¼	teaspoon Tabasco
2-4	tablespoons soy sauce	1	teaspoon ground black pepper
¼	cup white wine		cayenne pepper (optional, for hot jerky)

Combine all ingredients, except venison and peppers in large airtight container. Submerge venison in sauce, seal and marinate overnight in refrigerator. Lay venison strips on dehydrator tray, leaving ¼ to ½- inch gap for air to circulate. Sprinkle both sides heavily with black pepper and cayenne (if desired). Cook in dehydrator for 8 to 12 hours, rotating trays. The lower trays will be ready first.

Can store indefinitely in an airtight container placed in the refrigerator.

For conventional oven, lay jerky strips on top and middle racks. Place a pan or foil on bottom to catch drippings. Keep door open 1-inch to let moisture out. Bake at 150 to 170° for 5 to 6 hours.

Seared Scallopini of Nilgai

1	leg of nilgai, cut into scallops	1	teaspoon coriander seed, crushed
½	cup olive oil, divided	1	teaspoon thyme
1	pod garlic, peeled	¾	cup red wine
1	teaspoon salt	1	tablespoons chopped fresh rosemary
1	teaspoon cracked black pepper	4	tablespoons butter

Toss garlic cloves with ¼ cup olive oil. Spread on baking sheet and bake at 350° until golden brown, approximately 10 to 15 minutes. Combine next 4 ingredients and sprinkle over meat. In a large skillet heat remaining ¼ cup olive oil over high heat and sear meat, about 2 minutes each side. Remove meat and reduce heat to medium. Add red wine and reduce to about ½ cup. Add roasted garlic and rosemary and simmer for 1 minute. Stir in butter until melted. Pour over warm meat and serve immediately.

To prepare scallopini, cut the hind leg into long individual muscles. Remove any silver skin and sinuous parts. From the very lean muscle cut thin round slices, against the grain. This meat is very tender.

Caesar Kleberg imported this exotic antelope from India in the 1920s. They now range all over South Texas.

Game 169

Quail Stuffed with Oysters

2	dozen oysters, drained	salt and pepper	
¼	cup butter, melted	½	cup flour
1	cup bread crumbs	8	strips bacon
8	quail, cleaned		

Dip oysters in melted butter and roll in bread crumbs. Stuff each quail with 2 to 3 oysters. Brush quail with remaining butter, season with salt and pepper, and dust with flour. Place quail in a roasting pan and lay strips of bacon over the breasts. Bake at 350° for approximately 1½ hours, or until tender. Baste occasionally with pan juices.

Yield: 4 servings

All game birds should be picked, not skinned, while warm if possible.

Anne Armstrong's Eight Birds

8	quail or dove	1	teaspoon Beau Monde seasoning
2-3	tablespoons bacon drippings	⅓	cup sherry or Madeira wine
	salt	1	(14-ounce) can beef broth
	pepper	1	jalapeño, chopped
	thyme		
	flour		

Anne Armstrong was Ambassador to the Court of St. James.

Sprinkle birds with salt, pepper, and thyme. Dredge in flour. In a large skillet, brown birds in bacon drippings. Remove birds. Place Beau Monde seasoning, wine, bouillon, and jalapeño in same pan; bring to a boil. Return birds and cover; simmer 1 to 1½ hours. Serve with waffles, rice, or hot biscuits.

Yield: 4 to 6 servings

Quail in Wine Sauce

8	quail		pepper
2	tablespoons butter	¼	cup Cognac
2	tablespoons oil	1	cup dry white wine
1	small onion, minced	1	can condensed cream of
salt			chicken soup

Brown quail in oil. Add onion, salt, and pepper. Add warmed cognac and flame. Add wine and simmer until very tender, about 1 hour. If pan gets dry, add a small amount of chicken stock or more wine. A few minutes before serving, add soup and stir to blend.

Serve sauce over rice.

Yield: 4 servings

Two favorite recipes from "Fiesta", our first cookbook published in 1973.

Lasater's Mourning Doves

12	doves	2	cups water
3	tablespoons flour	1	cup dry white wine (or
½	cup butter		vermouth)
1	can condensed beef	2	chili pequins, crushed
	broth		

Flour doves and brown in butter in a heavy dutch oven. Add remaining ingredients, cover, and cook over an open fire for 2 hours. If preparing doves at home, cook at 350° for 2 hours 30 minutes. Add water if gravy becomes too thick.

Serve with rice or noodles.

Yield: 4 to 6 servings

Dove Kabobs

24	dove breasts, deboned	2	bell peppers, sliced
1	bottle Italian dressing	1	pound mushrooms,
2	medium onions,		halved
	quartered	1	pound bacon, sliced in
			2 inch strips

Marinate dove breasts in Italian dressing for 1 hour. Alternate onion, bell pepper, mushrooms, bacon, and dove on skewers. Make sure bacon is next to one side of dove breast. Grill over mesquite wood fire.

Yield: 6 servings

For sport and palate alike, both the mourning and the whitewing dove get high marks from hunters as well as chefs.

Orange Game Hens

4	Cornish game hens	½	stick butter
2	oranges, scrubbed, seeded, and sliced	2	tablespoons brandy (optional)
½	cup honey	1	tablespoon cornstarch
¼	cup soy sauce	¼	cup orange juice

Cover bottom of greased 9x13-inch baking dish with half of the orange slices. Stuff remaining slices into cavities of hens; place into baking dish. Heat honey, soy sauce, and butter in saucepan, until butter melts. Remove from heat and stir in brandy. Pour mixture over hens and bake at 400° for 1 hour, basting frequently. Remove hens and drain juices into saucepan. Dissolve cornstarch in slightly warmed orange juice and add to pan juices. Bring to a boil and continue to cook until slightly thick. Serve with hens.

Yield: 4 to 6 servings

Duck and Quail Pot Pie

Pie Crust

2¾ cups all purpose flour	6 tablespoons shortening
½ teaspoon salt	¼ cup ice water
1 teaspoon baking powder	

Sift together flour, salt and baking powder. Cut in shortening until crumbly. Add cold water until mixture sticks together. Do not overmix. Divide into 4 balls and roll out on floured surface. Place crusts in bottom of two 9-inch pie pans. Cover and chill top crusts until ready to use.

Yield: top and bottom crust for two 9-inch pies

A tantalizing pie from chef Patrick Smith of the Corpus Christi Town Club.

Filling

6 quail	1 poblano pepper, roasted, peeled, and diced
1 duck	1 (14-ounce) can diced tomatoes
2 tablespoons olive oil	
1 medium onion, chopped	4 tomatillos, husks removed and diced
¼ cup carrot, diced	
1 turnip, peeled and diced	2 tablespoons cornstarch, moistened with cold water
2 small potatoes, diced	
1 tablespoon chopped garlic	3 tablespoons chopped cilantro
2 tablespoons canned chilpotle pepper in adobo sauce, minced	salt and pepper to taste

Season quail and duck with salt and pepper. Roast quail for 45 minutes and duck for 1 hour at 375°. Remove meat from bone and cut into 1-inch cubes. Set aside. In a small saucepan, heat olive oil and sauté onion until soft. Add carrots, turnips, and potatoes and cook for 3 minutes. Add garlic, chilpotle pepper, and poblano pepper; sauté for 1 minute. Add tomatoes with juice and enough water to cover vegetables (about ½ cup). Add dissolved cornstarch and simmer 4 to 5 minutes, until sauce is thickened. Remove from heat and stir in duck, quail, and cilantro. Salt and pepper to taste. Place mixture in prepared pie crust and cover with top crust. Pierce several times with a knife and bake at 375° for 1 hour.

Yield: 2 pies

Emil's Pheasant in Wine

2	pheasants, whole or cut up	½	pound mushrooms, sliced
1	cup flour	1	teaspoon fresh rosemary
½	teaspoon salt	1	tablespoon chopped fresh parsley or
½	teaspoon pepper		1 teaspoon dried
4	strips bacon	1	teaspoon salt
1	clove garlic, minced	½	teaspoon pepper
2	tablespoons chopped onion	½	cup dry white wine
		½	cup water

The brushland of South Texas was the birthplace of the cowboy. He was the Spanish vaquero who carved a new way of life astride a horse on a dusty arid plain.

Mix flour, salt, and pepper; dredge pheasants in mixture. Cook bacon until crisp and remove from skillet. Brown pheasants in bacon drippings. Remove birds, place in a deep baking dish, and sprinkle with crumbled bacon. In same skillet, add all remaining ingredients except wine and water. Sauté until mushrooms are soft. Add wine and ½ cup water. Bring to a boil and simmer 3 minutes. Pour sauce over pheasants and bake at 300° until tender, about 2 hours.

Yield: 4 to 6 servings

Venison Chorizo

6	whole dried red chili peppers, seeded	2	tablespoons distilled white vinegar
4	ounces ground red chilies (hot)	5	teaspoons salt
2	pods garlic, separated, peeled and minced	1	teaspoon ground black pepper
3	tablespoons dried oregano	½	teaspoon ground cloves
		6	pounds ground venison

In saucepan, cover dried chilies with water and boil until soft. Drain, reserving liquid. Purée chilies with enough liquid to form a smooth paste. Combine ground chilies with next 6 ingredients. Mix with venison and fry a small piece to check seasoning. Refrigerate for 3 days or freeze until ready to use.

Yield: 6 pounds

Vegetables

Mexican Heritage

The founding of Corpus Christi is often attributed to Henry Lawrence Kinney, who in 1839 established a trading post in an area that would become part of the city. But the history of the coastal Bend's central city and, indeed, all of South Texas is inextricably tied to that of Mexico. Many of the Mexican-Americans who help make up the majority population in this region, can trace their ancestry back to Northern Spain. Spain ruled Mexico, of which Texas was a part, until 1821 and Spanish immigration to Northern Mexico and South Texas continued for years after that date. Spain had issued some Texas land grants to Americans in the 1700s, hoping that colonization would, for one thing, deter Indian attacks and encourage Spanish settlements. Thousands of Americans came to the area. By the 1830s, The Texas Revolution ended with the Battle of San Jacinto as Sam Houston and a force of volunteers defeated General Antonio Lopez de Santa Anna. By signing the Treaty of Velasco, Santa Anna agreed to move his army south of the Rio Grande. However, the land between the Rio Grande River and the Nueces River remained in dispute for another twelve years. In 1845, the United States voted Texas into the Union and prepared for war with Mexico as General Zachary Taylor led his troops through Corpus Christi and down south. The United States won the war and in 1848, the Treaty of Guadalupe Hidalgo established the Rio Grande as the new boundary of Texas. Much of the land that had been granted to or claimed by Mexicans was abandoned or sold as owners retreated south of the border. Kinney bought almost 40,000 acres from the Mexican soldier, Enrique Villarreal of Matamoros between 1840 and 1846. Much of South Texas land already was established and would continue to be worked in the Spanish ranching tradition.

¡VIVA! Tradiciones

Bird's Potatoes

¼ cup olive oil	1 cup seasoned bread
4 cloves garlic, minced	crumbs
6 cups peeled and cubed	½ cup Parmesan cheese
potatoes	salt and pepper to taste

Place olive oil and garlic in 9x13-inch casserole. Brown garlic in a 400° oven, about 3 minutes. Remove from oven and toss potatoes, bread crumbs, and Parmesan cheese in oil. Season with salt and pepper. Cover with foil and bake at 400° for 45 minutes. Uncover and brown potatoes for 15 minutes.

Yield: 8 servings

Garlic oven roasted potatoes that compliment any meal.

Lemon Dill Stuffed Potatoes

4 large baking potatoes,	⅓ cup sour cream
scrubbed	2 teaspoons dill weed
¼ cup butter	4 teaspoons lemon juice

Bake potatoes until tender. Cut potatoes in half and carefully scoop out insides, leaving peel intact. Combine potato pulp with remaining ingredients. Mound mixture in potato skins and bake at 400° until heated through, about 10 to 15 minutes.

Yield: 4 servings

Scalloped Sweet Potatoes

4 pounds sweet potatoes	¼ teaspoon white pepper
3 cups half & half	1 cup brown sugar
¼ teaspoon salt	

Peel potatoes and slice very thin. In heavy saucepan, combine potatoes, cream, salt, and pepper and bring to a quick boil. Remove from heat. Transfer to a buttered casserole dish and bake, covered, at 375° for 30 minutes. Sprinkle with brown sugar; bake uncovered, at 350° for 20 to 30 minutes.

Yield: 8 servings

A creamy but not too sweet version of sweet potatoes.

Potatoes Provençal

2	tablespoons olive oil	4	green onions, sliced
4	medium potatoes, baked and chopped	2	cloves garlic, minced
1	cup sliced zucchini	¼	cup chopped parsley
1	cup cubed red bell pepper		zest of 1 lemon
			salt and pepper to taste

Heat oil in non-stick skillet over medium-high heat; add potatoes and cook, turning frequently until lightly browned about, about 5 minutes. Add zucchini, bell pepper, onions, and garlic; cook, stirring, for 3 minutes. Stir in parsley and zest; season with salt and pepper.

Yield: 4 servings

Potatoes should never be stored in the refrigerator. The starch turns to sugar giving them an unusual taste.

Potatoes Pizzaiola

1	pound potatoes	½	teaspoon pepper
1	clove garlic, chopped	½	teaspoon oregano
½	red bell pepper, cut into strips	1	cup tomato juice
1	tablespoon olive oil	½	cup diced fresh tomatoes
½	teaspoon salt	1	cup grated mozzarella cheese

Cut unpeeled potatoes into ⅛-inch slices. Sauté next 3 ingredients in oil, stirring occasionally. Cook until potatoes are crisp-tender, about 5 minutes. Stir in seasonings, juice, and tomatoes. Cover and simmer over low heat until potatoes are soft, about 30 to 40 minutes. Remove from heat. Top with cheese and cover, let stand 1 to 2 minutes to melt cheese.

Yield: 4 servings

Grilled Potatoes

1	pound red or white potatoes, scrubbed
1½	pounds sweet potatoes, scrubbed
½	cup olive oil

1	tablespoon chopped parsley
1	tablespoon thyme
½	teaspoon salt
½	teaspoon pepper red pepper flakes

Cut potatoes in 1½-inch cubes. Steam potatoes over boiling water until almost tender, about 15 minutes. Remove from heat and cool. In a small bowl, combine olive oil, herbs and spices. Toss potatoes in herb mixture and marinate 30 minutes. Arrange on skewers and pour remaining marinade over. Grill, turning frequently, until browned, 10 to 15 minutes.

Yield:6 servings

Sweet potatoes are native to Mexico. Empanaditas are little fried pies with sweet potato filling.

Bourbon Sweet Potatoes

3	(29-ounce) cans sweet potatoes
¾	cup brown sugar
4	tablespoons margarine
1	teaspoon cinnamon
½	teaspoon cloves

½	teaspoon nutmeg
½	teaspoon allspice
	dash of salt
1½	cups bourbon
20-40	large marshmallows

Drain sweet potatoes, reserving 1 cup liquid, and mash. In a small bowl, combine ½ cup sweet potato liquid, brown sugar, margarine, spices and salt. Microwave on high 2 to 3 minutes, stirring after 1 minute. Add to sweet potatoes and blend until semi-smooth. Stir in bourbon. Add remaining sweet potato liquid. Place in a greased 9x13 casserole and bake at 350° for 20 minutes. Just before serving, add marshmallows; brown under broiler for 1 to 2 minutes. Watch carefully.

Yield: 12 servings

Even people who hate sweet potatoes will love this traditional holiday dish.

Tamale Dressing

1	cup chopped onion	1½	cups chopped parsley
1	cup chopped celery	1	(4-ounce) can chopped
¼	cup butter		green chilies
2	dozen pork or chicken	1	(14-ounce) can chicken
	tamales, chopped		broth

Sauté onion and celery in butter until soft. In a large bowl, combine tamales, parsley and onion mixture. Add chilies and enough chicken broth to moisten. Place in a 9x13-inch baking dish and bake at 375° for 30 to 45 minutes.

Homemade or fresh tamales are the best.

Yield: 12 servings

A quick and very popular holiday stuffing from Patrick Smith, chef at the Corpus Christi Town Club.

Spicy Couscous

1	(10-ounce) package uncooked couscous	1	(10-ounce) can diced tomatoes with green chilies
2½	cups chicken broth		
2	tablespoons butter	½	teaspoon dried basil
½	cup chopped onion	½	teaspoon dried oregano
2	cloves garlic minced	1	teaspoon salt
3	tablespoon olive oil	½	teaspoon red pepper
1	cup thinly sliced carrots		flakes, or to taste
1	bell pepper, seeded and chopped		

In a large saucepan bring broth and butter to boil. Stir in couscous and cover. Remove from heat and let stand 5 minutes. In a large skillet, sauté onion and garlic in oil. Add carrots and bell pepper. Sauté 5 minutes. Add tomatoes and spices. Simmer 5 minutes. Toss tomato mixture with couscous in a large bowl. Serve with a sprinkle of grated cheese, if desired.

This dish can also be made with meat or cut up chicken sautéed in the oil with onions.

Yield: 6 side servings

Barley Pilaf with Mushrooms

1 cup sliced fresh mushrooms	1 teaspoon lemon juice
½ cup chopped onion	½ teaspoon sea salt
2 tablespoons olive oil	⅛ teaspoon cayenne pepper
2 cups regular pearl barley	4 cups chicken broth
1 tablespoon snipped tarragon	

In a large oven proof skillet, sauté mushrooms and onion in oil until soft. Add next 5 ingredients and 2 cups chicken broth. Stir and bring to a boil. Cover and bake at 350° for 25 minutes. Uncover and stir in remaining chicken broth. Return to oven and bake, uncovered, 20 minutes until liquid is absorbed and barley is tender.

Table salt can be used instead of sea salt.

Yield: 8 servings

Pearl barley has been steamed before packaging and will not need to cook as long as regular medium barley.

Weird, Wonderful Rice

2 tablespoons margarine	1 cup sliced mushrooms
1 cup chopped celery	1 (5-ounce) package long grain wild rice
1 cup chopped onion	1 (14-ounce) can chicken broth
¾ cup chopped carrot	
½ cup chopped bell pepper	½ teaspoon salt
1 cup chopped Granny Smith apples	¼ cup slivered almonds, toasted

In large skillet, melt margarine; sauté celery, onion, carrot, and bell pepper, about 8 minutes. Add apple and mushrooms; sauté 2 more minutes. Add rice and mix well. Combine chicken broth with enough water to make 2 cups. Stir into rice with salt and bring to boil. Cover and lower heat. Cook about 10 minutes. Sprinkle with almonds immediately before serving.

Yield: 4 servings

A dish with character!

Red Pepper Rice

2	tablespoons olive oil	½	teaspoon cumin
½	cup chopped red bell pepper	1	cup converted rice
¼	cup chopped green onion	1½	cups vegetable broth
			salt and pepper to taste

Sauté red pepper and onion in oil until soft. Add cumin and rice; cook over low heat until rice is lightly browned. Add broth, salt, and pepper. Bring to a boil, cover, and lower heat. Simmer for 17 minutes; fluff with a fork.

Yield: 4 servings

Risotto alla Milanese

7	tablespoons butter, divided	3	cups arborio rice
1	small onion, thinly sliced	6½	cups beef broth, boiling
2	tablespoons bone marrow		large pinch of saffron, soaked in water
½	cup dry red or white wine	¾	cup Parmesan cheese

A family favorite from Marino of Mamma Mia's Restaurant.

Melt 3½ tablespoons butter in large pan. Sauté onion and bone marrow until onion is soft. Add wine; reduce by half. Stir in rice and sauté until golden. Add 1 cup of boiling stock and stir until liquid is absorbed. Add remaining boiling stock and stir until all liquid is absorbed, about 20 minutes. Add saffron and mix well. Remove from heat. Gently and thoroughly stir in remaining butter and Parmesan cheese. Cover pan and let stand for 2 minutes. Serve at once.

Extra Parmesan cheese for sprinkling is a must! This dish can be made with mushrooms, crawfish, sausage, and any other variation you can think of.

Yield: 6 main course servings

Ellen's Ratatouille Gratin

salt
1 medium eggplant, peeled and thinly sliced
4 tablespoons olive oil, divided
1 large onion, thinly sliced
1¼ cups Parmesan cheese, divided
3 medium tomatoes, peeled and sliced

1 clove garlic, minced
juice of 1 lemon
2 tablespoons chopped fresh basil
2 small zucchini, thinly sliced
1 large bell pepper, cut in 1-inch strips

Salt eggplant slices and place in a colander. Drain for 1 hour pressing out excess moisture. Coat a large skillet with oil. Cover bottom with layer of eggplant. Layer onion and sprinkle with Parmesan cheese. Add tomatoes and ½ of the garlic, ½ of the lemon juice and all of the basil. Next, layer zucchini, sprinkle with Parmesan cheese and top with remaining eggplant. Finish with a layer of onions, tomatoes, garlic, and lemon juice. Place bell pepper strips around edge of the dish; sprinkle with Parmesan cheese. Cover and simmer over low to medium heat for 20 minutes. Remove from heat and pour off any liquid. Place remaining cheese on top, and drizzle with remaining olive oil. Place under a broiler until the cheese is melted.

Yield: 4 servings

For a spicier taste, add 1 can diced Rotel tomatoes and green chilies on top of the tomato slices.

Corpus Christi boasts of having its own aircraft carrier in dry dock. The USS Lexington, or "Gray Ghost" sits in the harbor serving as a museum and touring facility.

Wild Rice Piquant

1 cup wild rice
2¾ cups water
¼ cup raisins
½ cup brandy
1⅓ cups finely diced carrots

⅔ cup finely diced celery
2 tablespoons butter, melted
1 teaspoon cinnamon

Bring water to a boil, add rice and cover. Reduce heat and cook 1 hour. In a small saucepan, combine raisins and brandy. Boil for 1 minute. Combine rice, raisins, and remaining ingredients. Transfer to ovenproof casserole and bake at 350° for 35 minutes.

Yield: 4 servings

Vegetables

Italian Stir-Fry Vegetables

2 tablespoons extra virgin olive oil	½ red or yellow bell pepper, cut in strips
½ small yellow onion, cut in strips	½ cup sliced zucchini
1 clove garlic, minced	½ cup sliced mushrooms
¼ teaspoon fresh ground pepper	2 small Roma tomatoes, cut in wedges
	¼ cup fresh basil, chopped
	dash of salt

Prepare all vegetables before heating oil in wok. Stir fry onion, garlic and black pepper in hot oil for 1 minute. Add bell pepper and zucchini; stir fry 1 minute. Add mushrooms; stir fry 1 minute. Add tomatoes, basil, and salt, and cook just until heated thoroughly. Serve immediately.

Yield: 4 servings

Roquefort Broccoli

1 (10-ounce) package frozen chopped broccoli	2 tablespoon Roquefort cheese or more to taste
1 tablespoon butter, melted	⅓ cup crushed Ritz crackers

Incredibly simple and deliciously fabulous!

Boil broccoli in salted water for 4 minutes. Drain and place in casserole. Top with butter, crumbled cheese, and cracker crumbs. Bake at 375° for 30 minutes.

Yield: 2 servings

Broccoli Vinaigrette

1½ pounds broccoli, cut in bite size pieces	3 tablespoons red wine vinegar
⅓ cup olive oil	1 teaspoon lemon pepper

Steam broccoli over 1 cup water for 7 minutes. In a small bowl, whisk together oil, vinegar, and lemon pepper. Toss broccoli with dressing and serve immediately.

Yield: 2 servings

Cauliflower and Broccoli Special

1   large head cauliflower,
    cut in florets
3   tablespoons Parmesan
    cheese
1   bunch broccoli, cut in
    florets

2   tablespoons butter
¼   cup sour cream
    salt and pepper to taste
⅓   cup bread crumbs

Boil cauliflower in salted water for 5 minutes; drain. Boil broccoli in salted water for 5 minutes; drain. Place cauliflower in a 2-quart casserole. Sprinkle with Parmesan cheese. Purée broccoli in a blender with butter and sour cream. Season broccoli mixture with salt and pepper and spoon over cauliflower. Top with bread crumbs. Bake at 350° for 20 minutes.

Yield: 8 servings

Cajun Cauliflower

    head cauliflower, cut into
    florets
½   bunch green onions,
    chopped
    tablespoons butter or
    margarine
    tablespoons flour
    teaspoon salt

1½ cups milk
4   ounces sharp Cheddar
    cheese, grated
½   roll garlic cheese, cubed
½   cup Rotel tomatoes,
    drained
    buttered Italian bread crumbs

Steam cauliflower until crisp-tender. Drain and place in a 2-quart casserole. In a saucepan, sauté onions in butter until soft. Stir in flour and salt. Add milk and stir until thick. Place in a blender with cheeses, tomatoes, and onions. Blend until smooth. Pour over cauliflower and top with bread crumbs. Bake at 350° until bubbly, about 20 minutes.

Yield: 6 to 8 servings

*Add more Rotel toma-
toes and green chilies if
you like it hot!*

Cauliflower Dijon

1	head cauliflower, cut in florets	¼	teaspoon salt
½	cup light mayonnaise	2	teaspoons Dijon mustard
		½	cup grated Cheddar cheese

Boil cauliflower in salted water for 10 to 12 minutes; drain. In a small bowl, mix mayonnaise, salt, and mustard. Toss with cauliflower and cheese.

Yield: 6 to 8 servings

Special Carrots

5	cups sliced carrots	¼	teaspoon salt
⅓	cup water	⅛	teaspoon pepper
1	tablespoon cornstarch	2	teaspoons chopped parsley
¾	cup orange juice		

Even carrot-haters will love this dish!

Boil carrots in water until crisp tender. Drain and reserve liquid. Set carrots aside. Dissolve cornstarch in orange juice, add to 3 tablespoons carrot liquid. Season with salt and pepper. Bring to a boil over medium heat, stirring constantly until thick. Add carrots and cook 1 minute, stirring well. Transfer to serving dish and garnish with parsley.

Yield: 8 servings

Lemon Basil Zucchini

3	medium zucchini	½	teaspoon lemon zest
2	tablespoons olive oil	¾	teaspoon chopped fresh basil
	juice of ½ lemon		

Cut zucchini into 2-inch pieces and then quarter each piece. Sauté zucchini in hot oil until crisp tender. Toss with lemon juice, zest, and basil.

To lower fat content, substitute ⅓ cup chicken broth for the oil.

Yield: 4 servings

Creole Zucchini

1	cup chopped onion	4	tomatoes, peeled and chopped
1	clove garlic, minced	½	teaspoon salt
⅓	cup chopped bell pepper	¼	teaspoon pepper
¼	cup salad oil	¼	cup chopped parsley
2	pounds zucchini, sliced	¼	cup Parmesan cheese

In skillet, sauté onion, garlic, and bell pepper in oil until soft. Add zucchini, tomatoes, salt and pepper. Cover and cook over medium heat for 20 minutes. Serve topped with parsley and Parmesan cheese.

Yield: 6 to 8 servings

John Andrew Wuensche introduced sorghum and the technology to farm and harvest this crop to South Texas in the early 1930's.

Grilled Zucchini

4	medium zucchini, halved lengthwise	2	tablespoons chopped parsley
¼	cup balsamic vinegar	¼	teaspoon granulated sugar
¼	cup olive oil		black pepper to taste

Place zucchini in glass dish. Combine remaining ingredients and pour over zucchini. Marinate 1 hour, turning once. Grill strips over hot coals until tender. Brush often with marinade. Sprinkle with extra parsley before serving.

Yield: 4 servings

Zucchini Parmesan

4	small zucchini, thinly sliced		dash of pepper
4	tablespoons butter	3	tablespoons Parmesan cheese
¼	teaspoon salt		

Sauté zucchini in butter for 5 minutes. Season with salt and pepper. Cover and cook 5 minutes more. Toss with cheese and serve immediately.

Yield: 4 to 6 servings

Baked Squash

Grandmother called this "corn dish" because her children didn't like squash but loved corn.

7	large yellow squash	10	slices white bread, crusts removed
2	medium white onions, chopped	1	cup milk
⅓	cup margarine	4	eggs, beaten
			salt and pepper to taste

Boil squash until tender, drain, and mash. In a large skillet, sauté onion in margarine. Soak bread in milk and squeeze out excess liquid. Add to onion and sauté until lightly browned. Combine bread mixture with squash and remaining ingredients. Place in a 9x13 casserole and bake at 350° for 1 hour.

Try adding green and red bell pepper for a jazzier color.

Yield: 8 servings

Stuffed Acorn Squash

3	acorn squash	4	cups shallots, chopped
2¼	cups vegetable broth	2	cloves garlic, minced
½	cup brown rice	1	tablespoon chopped parsley
¼	cup wild rice		
½	cup chopped celery	½	teaspoon crushed sage
¼	cup chopped mushrooms	½	teaspoon thyme
½	cup chopped carrots		

Prick squash with a fork and bake at 350° for 1 hour. While squash is cooking, prepare the stuffing. Bring 2 cups of broth to boil and add rices. Reduce heat, cover and cook for 40 minutes. In a separate pan, sauté celery and next 4 ingredients in ¼ cup broth until tender. Combine cooked rice with vegetable mixture and season with remaining ingredients. Add salt and pepper if desired. Cut cooled acorn squash in half and remove seeds. Fill each half with ½ cup of the stuffing. Serve immediately.

Yield: 6 servings

¡VIVA! Tradiciones

Squash Puppies

1½	cups sliced yellow squash	1	tablespoon baking powder
1	egg	½	teaspoon salt
⅓	cup flour	½	cup chopped onion
⅓	cup cornmeal		

Boil squash until tender; drain and mash. Combine squash with egg and set aside. Mix together flour, cornmeal, baking powder, and salt. Add chopped onions and blend well. Fold in squash mixture; it should cook like pancake batter. Drop by spoonfuls on a hot skillet coated with nonstick cooking spray. Cook until golden brown, turning once.

Yield: 2 dozen

Two Corn Casserole

½	cup margarine, melted	1	(15-ounce) can creamed corn
¼	bell pepper, chopped		
½	cup chopped onion	1	(8-ounce) box corn muffin mix
3	eggs, beaten		
	(15-ounce) can whole corn, undrained	1	cup grated Cheddar cheese

Combine all ingredients except cheese. Place in greased 9x13 casserole and top with cheese. Bake at 350° for 55 to 60 minutes. Let stand 5 minutes before serving.

Yield:12 servings

Add 1-2 chopped and seeded jalapeños and ½ teaspoon ground cumin for a Tex-Mex version.

Yvonne's Cornbread Dressing

1	cup margarine	2	teaspoons Accent
2	cups chopped celery	2	teaspoons poultry
1	medium onion, chopped		seasoning
	fine	2	teaspoons salt
2	cans chicken broth	2	teaspoons pepper
1	can cream of chicken	5	cups corn bread cubes
	soup	6	slices toasted bread,
1	tablespoon sage		cubed

This is a very moist, traditional Southern dressing. While cream of chicken soup may seem strange, it contributes to the dressing's success in being able to prepare it ahead of time and bake it in a casserole.

In large skillet, sauté celery and onion in margarine over low heat until soft. Add broth and soup; simmer 10 minutes. Combine remaining ingredients in a large bowl. Stir in liquid until very moist. Mixture should be dryer if used to stuff a turkey. Place in a greased shallow 3-quart casserole. May be refrigerated at this point. Mixture will keep for several days. Preheat oven to 350° and bake for 30 minutes until heated throughout. Baste with turkey drippings if dressing appears to be too dry.

Yield: 12 servings

Excellent Eggplant

1	large eggplant, halved	1	small zucchini, sliced
	lengthwise	½	teaspoon basil
2	tablespoons olive oil	½	cup Gruyère cheese,
1	onion, chopped		grated
1	clove garlic, chopped		pinch of sugar
2	large tomatoes, peeled		salt and pepper
	and diced		

Score flesh of eggplant in crisscross pattern. Brush with oil and place skin side up in a casserole dish. Bake at 400° for 40 minutes. Cool and remove skin, chop eggplant, and set aside. Sauté tomatoes, zucchini, and basil in hot oil for 20 minutes. Add eggplant and mix well. Add half the cheese and the sugar. Mix and season to taste. Place in a 2-quart casserole and top with remaining cheese. Bake at 375° for 20 minutes

Yield: 4 servings

Filetti di Melanzane

2	eggplants, peeled and sliced	4	cloves garlic, chopped
½	cup olive oil	¼	teaspoon onion powder (optional)
3	tablespoons chopped parsley		salt and pepper
1	tablespoon oregano	½	cup wine vinegar

Sauté eggplant in 2 tablespoons oil for 3 minutes each side; set aside. Combine parsley, oregano, garlic, onion powder, salt and pepper. Layer eggplant slices in glass bowl, topping each layer with herb mixture. Top with remaining oil and vinegar. Refrigerate overnight. Let stand for about 20 to 30 minutes before serving.

Yield: 6 servings

Small firm eggplants with a smooth tight skin are best. Large eggplants or those with brown spots can be bitter.

Eggplant Casserole

1	eggplant, peeled and sliced		salt and pepper
1	medium onion, sliced	2	cloves garlic, minced
1	medium tomato, sliced	2	tablespoons chopped chives
2	cups grated Mozzarella cheese		

In a greased casserole, layer eggplant and half of next 3 ingredients. Season with salt and pepper; repeat layers, ending with cheese. Sprinkle with garlic and chives. Bake, covered, at 350° for 45 minutes.

Yield: 6 servings

Brussels Sprouts and Artichokes Au Gratin

1	(10-ounce) package frozen Brussels sprouts	½	teaspoon celery salt
1	(14-ounce) can artichoke hearts, drained	¼	cup Parmesan cheese
½	cup mayonnaise	¼	cup butter
		2	teaspoons lemon juice

Cook Brussels sprouts in ½ cup water until just tender; drain. Arrange sprouts and artichokes in greased casserole. Combine remaining ingredients and spoon over sprouts. Bake uncovered at 425° for 8 to 10 minutes.

Yield: 6 servings

Use beaten egg whites in place of whole egg to lower fat.

Cuori di Carciofi al Forno (Baked Artichoke Hearts)

2	(14-ounce) cans artichoke hearts, drained	1	cup seasoned bread crumbs
		2	eggs, beaten

Cut artichoke hearts in half and dip in beaten egg. Roll in bread crumbs and place on greased pan. Bake at 325° for 25 minutes until browned.

Serve with marinara sauce for dipping.

Yield: 6 servings

Kimberly's Bueno Beans

1	pound pinto beans	3	cloves garlic, sliced
2	tablespoons chili powder		smoked turkey leg or wing
1	jalapeño, seeded and sliced	1	(14½-ounce) can tomatoes
1	medium onion, coarsely chopped	1	tablespoon granulated chicken or beef bouillon
			salt and pepper

Sort and rinse beans. Place in 6-quart saucepan and cover with water. Bring to boil, cover, and let simmer for 45 minutes. Add more water if needed and return to boil. Add remaining ingredients and cook 3 hours, or until tender. Salt and pepper to taste.

Canadian bacon may be substituted for smoked turkey.

Yield: 12 servings

There are frijoles of many colors. Try this wonderful recipe with the frijole color of your choice!

Dorothy's Black Beans

1	pound black beans		ham bone with trimmings
1	large onion, chopped	2	chicken bouillon cubes
6-8	cloves garlic, sliced	1-3	jalapeños, sliced and seeded
1½	tablespoons comino seed, crushed		

Rinse and sort beans. Place in a large Dutch oven with remaining ingredients. Cover with water 1-inch above beans. Bring to a rolling boil and transfer to oven. Bake at 325° for 3 to 4 hours, stirring occasionally, until tender.

Can use pepper-smoked bacon or smoked ham hocks instead of ham bone.

Yield: 8 servings

The Wiz's Red Beans and Rice

2 tablespoons bacon drippings or oil
4 green onions with tops, chopped
1 bell pepper, chopped
3 ribs celery, chopped
½ cup minced carrots
fresh oregano, rosemary and thyme, chopped -or- 1 tablespoon Italian seasonings
3 bay leaves
3 tablespoons chopped parsley
2 cloves garlic, minced
salt and pepper to taste
3 dashes Tabasco sauce
3 dashes Worcestershire sauce
1 (15-ounce) can chicken broth
1 pound package dry red beans, rinsed and sorted
1 pound ham, cut in chunks
1 ring sausage, sliced (not smoked)
cooked rice

In a heavy stock pot, sauté vegetables and seasonings in oil. Add broth, beans, and remaining ingredients. Add enough water to cover by 1-inch or more. Bring to a boil, cover, and simmer over low heat about 3 hours, stirring often. Remove about ½ cup beans and mash, return to pot to thicken juice. Continue cooking until meat is tender, about ½ hour. Adjust seasonings and serve over hot rice.

Camp's Venetian-style Spinach

1 pound fresh spinach, washed and stemmed
1½ tablespoons olive oil
1 clove garlic, thinly sliced
salt and pepper to taste

Sauté garlic and spinach in hot oil just until wilted. Salt and pepper to taste.

Yield: 4 servings

Claudia's Drunk Beans

2 cups dry pinto beans
2 teaspoons salt
1 cup chopped onion
2 cloves garlic
1 bay leaf
¼ teaspoon oregano
½ pound bacon
1½ cups bell pepper, chopped
2 teaspoons chili powder
1 cup sherry
3 tablespoons molasses
½ cup dry mustard

Sort and rinse beans. Place all ingredients in a large pot with enough water to cover. Cover pot and simmer over low heat until beans are tender, about 3 hours. Serve warm.

Soaking beans overnight will reduce cooking time to about 2 hours.

Garlic Spinach

3 cloves garlic, chopped	salt and pepper to taste
¼ cup olive oil	2 large tomatoes, sliced
1 (10-ounce) package frozen chopped spinach, thawed	¼ cup balsamic vinegar
	¼ cup Parmesan cheese

Sauté garlic in oil until lightly browned. Add spinach and sauté until thoroughly heated. Season with salt and pepper. Arrange tomatoes on plates; top with spinach. Drizzle with vinegar, and sprinkle with Parmesan cheese.

Sinfully simple!

Yield: 4 to 6 servings

Spinach Soufflé

2 (10-ounce) packages frozen chopped spinach, thawed and drained	1 cup grated mild Cheddar cheese
1 cup cottage cheese	2 eggs, slightly beaten
1 (8-ounce) package cream cheese, softened	Parmesan cheese

Combine all ingredients together except Parmesan cheese. Pour in greased casserole and top with Parmesan cheese. Bake at 350° for 45 minutes to 1 hour. Serve warm.

You may substitute fat free cottage cheese and cream cheese.

Yield:6 to 8 servings

Eddie's Black-eyed Peas

1	pound dried black-eyed peas, rinsed and sorted
½	pound center-cut ham, cut in ½-inch pieces
1	large onion, chopped
1	large bell pepper, chopped
2	stalks celery, chopped
3	medium jalapeños, seeded
1	(4-ounce) can sliced mushrooms, undrained
1	tablespoon Worcestershire sauce
1	teaspoon Tabasco sauce
	juice of ½ lime
1-2	teaspoons salt
1	teaspoon pepper

Mash black-eyed peas in a food processor with some of the juice from the crockpot and 1 to 2 tablespoons picante sauce for a dip to be served with corn chips.

Place onions, bell peppers and jalapeños in food processor and mince. Place all ingredients in large crock pot, add water to cover 3-inches deep. Cook all night on low heat. Cook on high for an additional 3 hours in the morning.

Can be cooked on stove top in 3 to 4 hours.

Easy Baked Spinach

2	(10-ounce) packages frozen chopped spinach, thawed
1	cup light sour cream
1	envelope vegetable soup mix
½	cup bread crumbs
2	tablespoons butter

Cook spinach according to package directions, drain, pressing out as much liquid as possible. Stir in sour cream and soup. Spoon in greased baking dish. Top with bread crumbs and drizzle butter over top. Bake at 350° for 20 minutes.

Yield: 6 servings

The Last Green Bean Casserole

4	cups green beans, trimmed	½	teaspoon pepper
1	cup butter or margarine	2	cups milk
¼	cup mushrooms, sliced	2	cups grated sharp Cheddar cheese
1	small yellow onion, minced		dash of Tabasco sauce (optional)
1	(8-ounce) can water chestnuts, sliced	½	cup almonds, slivered
¼	cup flour	1	can French-fried onion rings
½	teaspoon salt		

Promise!

Boil beans until crisp tender. Melt butter in large, heavy skillet or Dutch oven. Sauté mushrooms, onion, and water chestnuts until translucent. Stir in flour, salt, and pepper, until smooth and thick. Add milk, stirring constantly, until smooth. Add cheese and stir until cheese is melted and sauce is very thick. Season with Tabasco. In 3-quart casserole, place ½ the beans, then ½ of the sauce; repeat. Top with almonds. Bake at 375°, uncovered, for 25 minutes. Sprinkle with onion rings and cook 5 minutes longer.

Soy sauce or Worcestershire sauce can be substituted for the Tabasco.

Yield: 8 to 12 servings

Wheel's Marinated Tomatoes

3	large tomatoes, sliced thick	olive oil
6-8	slices of Provolone cheese	fresh basil pepper

Place tomatoes on serving platter. Cut Provolone to fit over each tomato slice. Drizzle with olive oil. Place sprig of basil on top and sprinkle with fresh pepper. Refrigerate until ready to serve.

Yield: 6 to 8 servings

For best results, use fresh summer tomatoes, preferably grown from your own garden.

Italian Green Beans

2½	pounds green beans	½	teaspoon dried whole basil
⅓	cup olive oil		
1	cup sliced mushrooms	½	teaspoon Italian seasoning
⅓	cup chopped onion		
3	cloves garlic, crushed	1	(8-ounce) can sliced water chestnuts, drained
½	teaspoon salt		
1	tablespoon bell pepper	¼	cup Parmesan cheese

Boil green beans in water until crisp tender, about 8 minutes. Drain. In a large skillet, sauté mushrooms with next 6 ingredients. Stir in beans and water chestnuts and heat through. Sprinkle with Parmesan cheese.

Yield: 8 to 10 servings

Baked Tomato Slices

*fresh tomatoes
celery, chopped
onion, minced
brown or white sugar
butter*

Slice tomatoes ½-inch thick; do not peel . Place on lightly greased baking sheet, in 1 layer. On each slice place 1 teaspoon celery, 1 teaspoon onion, 1 teaspoon sugar and 1 pat butter. Bake at 300° for 1 hour or until desired degree of tenderness.

French Sautéed Mushrooms

3	tablespoons olive oil	¼	cup chopped parsley
4	tablespoons minced green onion		salt and pepper
		¼	teaspoon ground thyme
2	large cloves garlic, minced	¼	cup dry vermouth
1	pound mushrooms, sliced	¼	cup seasoned bread crumbs

Sauté onion, garlic, mushrooms and parsley in oil until soft. Season with salt, pepper and thyme. Add vermouth and continue to sauté until liquid is almost completely absorbed. Remove from heat and sprinkle with crumbs, toss, and serve.

Yield: 4 servings

Desserts

Junior League History

The Junior League of Corpus Christi has been changing our community for over 50 years. The primary focus of our work is to improve the lives of the children of our area through educational and service projects. We have been instrumental in many of the assets our community boasts today. Too many to list, but, this group of trained and dedicated women have seen a need in the community again and again and have thrived to fulfill it. The biggest success stories include: The Creative Arts Center, Kids Place, Casa, Texas Scholars, Heritage Park and in the recent years, a program called Postponing Sexual Involvement (P.S.I.). Collectively we can improve the lives of the children and be a catalyst for positive change. The proceeds from ¡VIVA! Tradiciones go directly to support the projects of The Junior League of Corpus Christi, making it possible for the continued charity of voluntarism that will endure to make a difference.

¡VIVA! Tradiciones

Kahlúa Espresso Cake

Cake

½ cup Kahlúa	4 eggs
4 tablespoons cocoa	½ teaspoon salt
1 teaspoon Mexican vanilla	1 cup buttermilk
½ cup shortening	1 tablespoon white vinegar
1½ cups sugar	1 teaspoon baking soda
2¼ cups unbleached flour, sifted	

Icing

½ cup butter, softened	1 tablespoon espresso or very strong coffee
1 (8-ounce) package cream cheese, softened	½ cup Kahlúa
1 (16-ounce) box powdered sugar, sifted	3 ounces bittersweet chocolate, grated

To prepare cake: combine first 3 ingredients to form a paste; set aside. Cream shortening with sugar and eggs one at a time. Slowly mix in Kahlúa paste. Blend flour into mixture 1 tablespoon at a time. Add remaining ingredients. Pour batter into 3 prepared 8-inch cake pans. Bake at 350° for 25 to 27 minutes. Stagger cake pans in oven for even heating. Be careful not to overbake! After removing from oven, let cool slightly in pans. Remove from pans and wrap each layer in plastic wrap while still warm to allow "sweating" to occur. This will give you a very moist cake. Remove plastic and generously brush each layer with Kahlúa on tops and sides. While layers are absorbing liquid, prepare icing.

To prepare icing: blend butter and cream cheese. Slowly add powdered sugar. Mix in espresso. As cake is iced, lightly sprinkle grated chocolate between each layer. Garnish top with remaining chocolate.

For a more "decorative" look, try making chocolate curls for the top of this divine creation.

Yield: 12 servings

Chocolate Truffle Cake with Praline Sauce

Cake

10	ounces semi-sweet chocolate	1	cup sugar
1	cup butter	1	tablespoon vanilla
5	eggs	3	tablespoons flour
		1	teaspoon baking powder

Praline Sauce

1¼	cups brown sugar	½	cup half & half
¾	cup light corn syrup	1	teaspoon vanilla
¼	cup melted butter	1½	cups roasted pecans
3	tablespoons flour		

A fun, easy way to serve coffee is to offer guests a selection of liqueur filled chocolates, whipped cream, sugar, and honey.

Grease and flour a 9-inch spring form pan. Melt chocolate and butter over low heat until smooth. In large bowl, beat eggs and sugar until light colored. Add vanilla, flour, and baking powder. Slowly stir in chocolate mixture and mix well. Pour in prepared pan and bake at 350° for 40 minutes. Remove from oven and cool. Center will fall leaving a lip around edge to hold sauce. To prepare Praline Sauce: melt brown sugar, syrup, and butter over medium heat. Stir in flour and cook for 5 minutes, stirring constantly. Add cream and vanilla, stir and bring to quick boil. Remove from heat and stir in pecans. Pour over cake or serve warm over individual slices.

Yield: 12 servings

Toffee Nut Pear Cake

2	cups light brown sugar	4	firm pears, cored and sliced
2	cups flour		
1	tablespoon cinnamon	1½	teaspoons baking soda
⅛	teaspoon nutmeg	1	egg
¼	teaspoon salt	1	cup sour cream
½	cup butter	1	cup chopped nuts

Combine sugar and next 4 ingredients. Cut in butter until mixture resembles cornmeal. Press ⅓ of mixture into bottom of 8-inch springform pan. Place pears on top. Mix baking soda, egg, and sour cream. Add to remaining dry ingredients and pour over pears. Sprinkle with nuts. Bake at 350° for 1 hour.

Yield: 12 servings

Fabulous Lemon Cake

Cake
1	Lemon Supreme cake mix	¼	cup lemon juice
1	(3½-ounce) box instant lemon pudding	4	eggs
		½	teaspoon lemon extract
		⅔	cup applesauce

Glaze
⅓	cup lemon juice	½	teaspoon lemon extract
1	teaspoon grated lemon zest	1¼	cups powdered sugar, sifted

Beat cake mix with next 5 ingredients for 2 minutes using electric mixer. Pour batter into greased and floured bundt pan. Bake at 350° for 45 minutes or until golden brown. For glaze, whisk all glaze ingredients until smooth. Invert cooled cake on plate. Poke holes in warm cake with a skewer. Pour glaze on top.

Fresh mint leaves and seasonal berries garnish beautifully.

Yield: 12 servings

Tia Maria Torte

24	ladyfingers	½	cup sugar
4	teaspoons instant espresso	3	tablespoons Tia Maria
1	tablespoon hot water	1	cup whipping cream
4	eggs		Raspberry Sauce page 222

Cut ladyfingers to fit bottom and up sides of buttered 9-inch springform pan. Set aside. Dissolve espresso in hot water. Set aside. Beat eggs until light. Gradually add sugar. Place in top of double boiler and cook over boiling water, stirring constantly for about 5 minutes. Remove from hot water and continue to beat until cooled. Beat in coffee paste. In separate bowl, whip cream until stiff peaks form and fold in Tía Maria. Fold in egg mixture and pour into prepared pan. Refrigerate 24 hours. Run knife along edges of pan and release sides. Serve with Raspberry Sauce on page 222.

Cut ladyfingers in half to form scallop edges along sides.

Yield: 10 servings

People come from near and far to participate in the annual Port Aransas Deep Sea Roundup fishing tournament started in 1954.

Truly Chocolate Cheesecake

⅓ cup butter or margarine, melted
1¼ cups graham cracker crumbs
¼ cup sugar
3 (8-ounce) packages cream cheese, softened

1 (14-ounce) can sweetened condensed milk
1 (12-ounce) package semi-sweet chocolate chips, melted
4 eggs
2 teaspoons vanilla

Combine butter, crumbs, and sugar. Press in bottom of 9-inch spring form pan. In a large mixing bowl or food processor, beat cream cheese until fluffy. Add condensed milk and beat until smooth. Add remaining ingredients and mix well. Pour into pan. Bake at 300° for 65 minutes or until center is set. Cool to room temperature. Remove side of pan. Keep in refrigerator until ready to serve.

Melt chocolate chips with condensed milk in microwave on 50% power

Yield: 12 servings

Splurge! Worth every calorie.

Chocolate Mint Cheesecake

Follow instructions for Truly Chocolate Cheese-cake substituting 1 tea-spoon peppermint ex-tract for 1 of the tea-spoons of vanilla extract. Bake for 50 minutes. Re-move from oven and top with sour cream mint topping and bake 15 minutes longer.

Sour Cream Mint Topping

2 cups sour cream
½ cup sugar
4 drops green food coloring

Mix and pour over baked cheesecake 15 minutes before removing from oven.

Strawberry Trifle

6-8 egg whites
½ box powdered sugar
1 teaspoon vanilla
2 (16-ounce) cartons sour cream

3 dozen ladyfingers
2-3 pints fresh strawberries, sliced

Beat egg whites until foamy. Add sugar and vanilla; beat until stiff peaks form. Fold in sour cream. Arrange 1 layer ladyfingers in bottom of glass trifle bowl. Pour ⅓ of cream mixture over ladyfingers. Place another layer of ladyfingers and then a layer of strawberries. Continue layering, ending with cream mixture. Chill several hours before serving

Use whole strawberries and fresh mint leaves for garnish.

¡VIVA! Tradiciones

Sinful Surprise Cheesecake

Crust

1½ cups vanilla wafer crumbs
1½ cups powdered sugar
½ cup finely chopped pecans
⅓ cup cocoa
⅓ cup butter or margarine, melted

Chocolate Pecan Cookie Dough

¼ cup butter or margarine, softened
¼ cup packed light brown sugar
¼ cup sugar
⅓ cup cocoa
2 tablespoons water
1 teaspoon vanilla extract
½ cup all-purpose flour
½ cup coarsely chopped pecans

Cheesecake batter

3 (8-ounce) packages of cream cheese, softened
1 (14-ounce) can sweetened condensed milk
3 eggs
1 teaspoon vanilla extract

Chocolate Drizzle

¼ cup semi-sweet chocolate chips
¼ teaspoon shortening (not oil)

Remarkably unforgettable and absolutely delicious!

Preheat oven to 300°. To make crust: combine all crust ingredients and press firmly in bottom and up sides of 9-inch spring form pan; set aside. To make dough: cream sugars with butter. Add cocoa and mix well. Stir in water and vanilla. Slowly add flour, mixing well. Stir in pecans. To make cheesecake batter: in a large mixing bowl, beat cream cheese until fluffy. Gradually mix in sweetened condensed milk until smooth. Add eggs and vanilla; beat well. Pour half of batter over prepared crust. Drop cookie dough by the teaspoon evenly over batter. Top with remaining batter. Bake 55 to 60 minutes or until center is set. Remove from oven and cool completely. Run a knife around edges of pan and remove sides. To make drizzle: in small microwave-safe bowl, place chocolate chips and shortening. Microwave on high for 45 seconds or until chips are completely melted when stirred. Drizzle over cake in lattice fashion. Refrigerate.

Place a whole pecan, half dipped in chocolate, at edge of each slice.

Yield: 12 servings

Butterscotch Cream Pie

6	tablespoons flour	4	tablespoons butter or
¾	cup brown sugar		margarine, melted
½	teaspoon salt	2	eggs
½	cup sugar	1	(9-inch) pie shell, baked
⅓	cup hot water	1	cup heavy cream,
2	cups milk		whipped
			slivered almonds, toasted

Pie Crust

3 cups flour
1¼ cups shortening
dash of salt
1 egg
1 tablespoon vinegar
⅓ cup cold water

Combine all ingredients in food processor until ball forms. Divide into four portions and refrigerate 15 minutes. Roll each ball out on a lightly floured surface. Place in pie pan.

Makes 4 crusts. Freeze unused crusts.

Combine first 3 ingredients and set aside. Place white sugar in a heavy saucepan and cook over medium heat, without stirring, until melted and golden brown. Remove from heat and slowly add to hot water. Stir until sugar dissolves. Add milk and heat to almost boiling, remove from heat. In top of double boiler, melt butter. Add flour mixture and mix well. Beat in eggs. Slowly add caramel mixture and cook over boiling water until thickened, stirring constantly. Cover and cook 10 additional minutes, stirring occasionally. Cool to room temperature and pour into pie shell. Chill several hours. Spread with whipped cream and sprinkle with nuts.

Yield: 8 servings

White Coconut Pie

1	tablespoon gelatin	1	cup heavy cream,
¼	cup cold water		whipped
1	cup sugar, divided	3	egg whites
4	tablespoons flour	¼	teaspoon cream of tartar
½	teaspoon salt	1	cup grated coconut
1½	cups milk	¼	cup fresh coconut
¾	teaspoon vanilla	1	(9-inch) pie crust, baked
¼	teaspoon almond extract		and cooled

This pie is stark white. It is beautiful garnished with green and red fruit for Christmas or frosted grapes for Easter.

Soften gelatin in water. Combine ½ cup sugar and next 3 ingredients in top of a double boiler. Stir until thick. Remove from heat and stir in gelatin. Cool in refrigerator until partially set, about 1 hour. Remove from refrigerator and beat until smooth. Add vanilla and almond extracts. Fold in whipped cream. In separate bowl, beat egg whites with cream of tartar slowly add and ½ cup sugar until stiff. Carefully fold in first mixture. Fold in grated coconut. Pour into pie crust. Sprinkle with fresh coconut. Chill in refrigerator 3 hours or overnight.

If garnishing with holly or ivy, dip cut ends in paraffin before placing on or around food.

Yield: 8 servings

Black Bottom Banana Pie

1½ cups graham cracker crumbs	2 (3-ounce) packages instant banana pudding
3 tablespoons butter, melted	1 (3-ounce) package cream cheese
4 ounces semi-sweet baking chocolate	1½ cups light whipped topping
2 tablespoons milk	2 bananas, sliced
2⅔ cups milk	1 cup sliced strawberries

May also use lowfat and sugar-free products.

Combine crumbs and butter. Press into a 9-inch pie pan. Bake at 350° for 15 minutes, and let cool. Microwave chocolate with 2 tablespoons milk on high for 1 to 1½ minutes, stirring every 30 seconds, until chocolate is melted and smooth. Spread evenly over pie crust and refrigerate. In a large bowl, combine 2⅔ cups milk with pudding mix. Beat for 1 minute. In separate bowl, beat cream cheese until smooth. Add whipped topping and mix until smooth. Fold cream cheese mixture into pudding mixture. Arrange bananas and strawberries over chocolate. Spoon pudding mixture over fruit. Refrigerate 4 hours before serving.

Garnish with sliced bananas, strawberries, or shaved chocolate.

Yield: 8 servings

Bourbon Chocolate Pecan Pie

3 eggs, beaten	2 tablespoons plus 1 teaspoon bourbon
1 cup sugar	
¾ cup light corn syrup	½ cup mini semi-sweet chocolate chips
¼ cup margarine, melted	
¼ teaspoon salt	1 (9-inch) pie shell, unbaked
3 teaspoons vanilla	
½ cup chopped pecans	

Combine first 6 ingredients, mixing well. Stir in pecans and next 2 ingredients. Pour into pastry shell. Bake at 375° for 55 to 60 minutes.

Freezes well.

Yield: 8 servings

Pralines and Cream Pie

1	cup evaporated milk	3	tablespoons flour
4	eggs	1	teaspoon vanilla
⅓	cup butter or margarine, melted	1½	cups pecans, coarsely chopped
1	cup sugar	1	(9-inch) pie shell, unbaked
¾	cup light brown sugar		

Process first 7 ingredients in a blender until smooth. Stir in pecans. Pour into pie crust and bake at 350° for 30 to 40 minutes, or until knife comes out clean. Cool completely before slicing.

Serve with whipped cream or ice cream.

Yield: 8 servings

Colonel Henry Kinney held the first State Fair in Corpus Christi on May 1, 1852. Prizes were silver urns, pitchers, goblets, and punch bowls from the Lone Star State Fair Committee.

Peach of a Berry Pie

1	(8-ounce) package cream cheese, softened	2	tablespoons cornstarch
3	tablespoons sugar	1½	cups chopped strawberries
¼	teaspoon salt	2	tablespoons lemon juice
1	tablespoon milk	3	peaches, peeled and sliced thin
½	teaspoon vanilla	1	(9-inch) pie crust, baked
¾	cup sugar		

Blend cream cheese with next 4 ingredients. Place in pie shell and spread to outer edges. Combine sugar with next 3 ingredients and cook over medium heat until thick. Spoon one-half of strawberry mixture into pie shell. Arrange peach halves around pie. Top with remaining strawberry mixture. Refrigerate 3 hours before serving.

Sliced pears can replace peaches

Yield: 8 servings

¡VIVA! Tradiciones

Deep in the Heart Plum Cobbler

Filling
5	cups sliced firm red or black plums	2	tablespoons tapioca
½	cup sugar	1	teaspoon cinnamon

Crust
1	cup flour	3	tablespoons butter, chilled and sliced
3	tablespoons sugar		
1	teaspoon baking powder	½	cup heavy cream

Topping
1	egg, beaten	1	teaspoon cinnamon
2	tablespoons sugar		

Toss fruit with sugar, tapioca, and cinnamon. To prepare crust: combine dry ingredients. Cut in butter until crumbly. Slowly add cream until dough forms. Roll out on floured surface to ¼-inch thickness. Place one-third of dough in bottom of a greased 8x12 glass pan. Top with fruit mixture. Cut remaining dough in 2-inch wide strips and create your own pattern on top of fruit. Brush dough with egg and sprinkle with sugar and cinnamon. Bake at 350° for 45 minutes. Serve warm.

Cut dough in heart shapes with cookie cutter.

Yield: 12 servings

Zesty Apple Crumble

7	cups apples, peeled and sliced	½	teaspoon nutmeg
⅓	cup fresh orange juice	½	teaspoon cinnamon
½	cup brown sugar	¼	teaspoon salt
½	cup sugar	¾	cup flour
2	teaspoons orange zest	½	cup margarine

Place apples in lightly greased deep pie pan or 1½-quart glass casserole. Pour orange juice over apples. In a bowl, combine brown sugar with next 6 ingredients. Cut in margarine until crumbly. Sprinkle mixture evenly over apples. Bake at 350° for 1 hour. Serve warm or cold.

Grandma's favorite topped with ice cream or yogurt.

Yield: 8 servings

Good as good can be!

Brice's Cookies

1	cup powdered sugar	2	teaspoons vanilla
1	cup sugar	5	cups flour
1	cup butter, softened (do not substitute)	1	teaspoon baking soda
		1	teaspoon cream of tartar
1	cup vegetable oil	¼	teaspoon salt
2	eggs, beaten		

Cream sugars with butter. Add oil and egg. in separate bowl, sift together dry ingredients. Gradually mix in flour. Form into 1-inch balls and place on ungreased cookie sheet. Flatten with decorative cookie stamp or fork. Sprinkle with sugar and bake at 350° for 10 to 12 minutes.

Yield: 7 dozen cookies

The best sugar cookies you will ever eat ... even before baking!

Persian Sugar Cookies

1	cup unsalted butter	1	teaspoon lemon extract
1	cup sugar	2	cups sifted flour
2	egg yolks (or 1 egg)	1	teaspoon baking powder
1	teaspoon vanilla		colored or plain sugar (optional)
1	teaspoon almond extract		

Cream butter and sugar. Add egg and flavorings. In separate bowl, sift flour with baking soda. Gradually add to sugar mixture and mix well. Refrigerate until firm. Form into 1-inch balls and place on ungreased cookie sheet. Flatten with fork and sprinkle with sugar. Bake at 300° for 20 to 25 minutes, or until edges turn brown. Cool and store in sealed container.

Yield: 6 dozen

Jon's Orange Gingersnaps

1	cup butter, softened	2	teaspoons ground cinnamon
1½	cups sugar		
1	egg	2	teaspoons ground ginger
2	tablespoons light corn syrup	½	teaspoon ground cloves
		2	tablespoons orange zest
3	cups flour	¼	cup orange juice
2	teaspoons baking soda		

Cream butter with next 3 ingredients. Sift dry ingredients and add to butter mixture. Add orange zest, juice, and mix well. Refrigerate dough for 2 hours. Drop by ½ teaspoon on greased baking sheet, about 1-inch apart. Bake at 375° for 8 to 10 minutes. Watch closely as they burn easily. Cool and store in airtight container.

This cookie may be rolled on a floured surface and cut with floured cookie cutters for special holidays. Decorate with sugar sprinkles or icing.

Yield: 7 to 8 dozen

Stores well for weeks sealed in airtight container … if they last that long.

Lazy Day Spice Cookies

1	box spice cake mix	1	teaspoon vanilla
2	cups oats	1	cup vegetable oil
2	eggs	1	cup chopped pecans
½	cup brown sugar, packed		raisins (optional)
1	teaspoon baking soda		

Combine all ingredients with mixer or by hand. Drop on ungreased baking sheet. Bake at 350° for 10 to 12 minutes. Cool and store in airtight container.

Yield: 5 dozen

These disappear quickly! You might want to double the recipe.

Texas Cowboy Cookies

2½	cups margarine, softened	2½	teaspoons vanilla
2¼	cups sugar	4½	cups quick oats
2¼	cups brown sugar	2	cups chopped pecans
5	eggs	1	(12-ounce) package semi-
4½	cups flour		sweet chocolate chips
2½	teaspoons baking soda	1	(12-ounce) package
1¼	teaspoons salt		butterscotch morsels

This makes a big batch! Perfect for feeding the whole herd.

In a large bowl, cream margarine and sugars. Add eggs and mix well. In separate bowl, combine dry ingredients and slowly add to sugar mixture. Add vanilla. Fold in oats, nuts, and chips. Refrigerate for a 2 hours. Drop by teaspoon on ungreased baking sheets. Bake at 350° for 10 to 12 minutes.

Dough can be divided in half and refrigerated for 2 weeks.

Yield: 10 to 13 dozen

Lorie's Double Chocolate Cookies

1	cup shortening	1	teaspoon baking soda
¾	cup sugar	1	teaspoon hot water
¾	cup brown sugar	2	cups quick oats
2	eggs	1	cup chopped nuts
1	teaspoon vanilla	1	cup semi-sweet
1½	cups flour		chocolate chips
¼	cup cocoa	½	cup coconut (optional)
1	teaspoon salt		

Cream shortening and sugars. Add eggs one at a time. Add vanilla. In separate bowl, combine flour and next 3 ingredients. Slowly add to sugar mixture. Stir in hot water and next 4 ingredients. Drop on greased baking sheets. Bake at 350° for 10 to 12 minutes.

Yield: 6 to 8 dozen

Pan de Polvo

3	cinnamon sticks	3	tablespoons cinnamon, divided
1	cup boiling water		
2½	cups sugar	2⅔	tablespoons granulated yeast
3	pounds shortening		
1	tablespoon Mexican vanilla	5	pounds, plus 1½ cups flour
		1	cup sugar

Preheat oven to 400°. Place cinnamon sticks in boiling water and set aside. Cream 2½ cups sugar with shortening and vanilla. Remove cinnamon sticks and place 1 teaspoon cinnamon and yeast in cinnamon water. Slowly add to sugar mixture. Gradually add flour and mix well. Divide dough in half and roll on a lightly floured surface. Cut in desired shapes and place on ungreased cookie sheet. Gather and roll leftover dough. Bake at 400° for 7 to 10 minutes. Cool and toss cookies in 1 cup sugar mixed with remaining cinnamon.

A cookie gun is very handy for these. Leftover dough can be frozen for 1 month.

Yield: Hundreds of small cookies.

Pan de Polvo or Mexican Wedding Cookies are always present at quinceneras, weddings, and holiday gatherings. This traditional cookie simply melts in your mouth.

Claudia's Shortbread

	cup butter or margarine, softened	2	cups flour
	box light brown sugar	1	teaspoon vanilla
	eggs	1	cup chopped nuts

Cream butter and sugar. Add remaining ingredients in order given. Spread dough in a greased 9x13 pan. Bake at 350° for 25 minutes. Cut in bars and cool.

Yield: 36 bars

A delightful change from the usual lemon bar!

Mexican Lime Bars

Crust

2	cups flour	1	cup butter
½	cup powdered sugar	½	teaspoon salt

Topping

4	eggs	½	teaspoon baking powder
⅓	cup lime juice	1	drop green food coloring,
¼	cup flour		optional
2	cups sugar		powdered sugar
1	teaspoon grated lime zest		

Combine flour and next 3 ingredients with a fork. Press mixture in a greased 9x13 baking dish. Bake at 350° for 20 to 25 minutes or until lightly browned. Beat eggs with lime juice. Stir in flour, sugar, zest, and baking powder. Add food coloring, if desired. Mix well. Pour over crust and bake at 350° for 25 minutes. Remove from oven and allow to cool. Sprinkle with powdered sugar before cutting.

Use Key limes if available.

Yield: 36 bars

Unknown Bars

1	(12-ounce) package semi-sweet chocolate chips	1	cup chopped nuts (optional)
1	(14-ounce) can sweetened condensed milk	1	cup margarine
		2	cups sugar
2	tablespoons butter	2	eggs
½	teaspoon salt	3	cups quick oats
4	teaspoons vanilla (divided)	2½	cups flour
		1	teaspoon baking soda

In a saucepan, over low heat, melt chocolate chips with milk, butter, salt, and 2 teaspoons vanilla. Add nuts if desired. Cool and set aside. Cream margarine and sugar; add eggs and 2 teaspoons vanilla. Add remaining ingredients except chocolate. Press ⅔ of flour mixture in 9x13 pan and pour on chocolate mixture. Pour chocolate mixture over Sprinkle rest of flour mixture on top. Bake at 350° for 25 to 30 minutes

Yield: 30 bars

Cream Cheese Bars

Crust

1½	cups flour	½	teaspoon cinnamon
1	cup brown sugar, firmly packed	⅔	cup butter or margarine, softened

Topping

2	tablespoons flour	1	(12-ounce) package semi-sweet chocolate chips (divided)
1	(8-ounce) package cream cheese, softened		
¼	cup sugar	¾	cup chopped walnuts or pecans
2	eggs, room temperature		

For crust: in a large bowl, combine flour with next 3 ingredients. Mix at medium speed until crumbly. Press in a 9x13 baking dish. Bake at 350° for 12 minutes. For topping: in a medium bowl, beat flour with next 3 ingredients until smooth, about 2 minutes. Stir in 1 cup chocolate chips. Pour over partially baked crust. Bake an additional 15 to 20 minutes, or until topping is almost set. Remove from oven and immediately sprinkle remaining chocolate chips over top. Return to oven for 1 minute to melt chips. Gently spread melted chocolate over top. Sprinkle with nuts and lightly press into chocolate. Refrigerate 1 hour and cut in bars. Refrigerate.

If bars get too cold they will be hard to cut.

Yield: 36 bars

Bunuelos

2 cups flour
2 tablespoons sugar
½ teaspoon salt
2 eggs
⅓ cup milk
2 tablespoons butter, melted
oil

Combine flour, sugar, and salt. Mix together milk and eggs; add butter. Combine with flour mixture just until wet. Knead dough 5 minutes and divide in 24 pieces. Roll out on a lightly floured surface. Drop each tortilla in hot oil and fry until golden brown. Drain and sprinkle with cinnamon and sugar.

Toffee Pecan Bars

2	cups flour		1	egg
½	cup powdered sugar		1	teaspoon vanilla
1	cup butter		1	cup toffee pieces
1	(14-ounce) can sweetened condensed milk		1	cup chopped pecans

Preheat oven to 350°. Combine flour and sugar. Cut in butter until mixture is crumbly. Press mixture in bottom of 9x13 glass pan. Bake for 15 minutes. In a mixing bowl, combine condensed milk with egg and vanilla. Stir in toffee and nuts. Spread evenly over crust and bake for 25 minutes or until golden brown. Cool and cut in bars. Store in sealed container.

Yield: 36 bars

Sweet Treats

Crust

1	cup unsalted butter, softened		1⅔	cups brown sugar
			1⅔	cups flour

Topping

1	cup brown sugar		2	cups chopped walnuts
4	eggs, lightly beaten		1	cup coconut
2	tablespoons flour			

For crust: cream butter and sugar. Add flour and mix well. Pat crust mixture evenly into a greased 9x13 glass pan. Bake at 350° for 15 to 20 minutes, until lightly brown. For topping: in a medium-size bowl, combine sugar and eggs. Add flour and mix well. Fold in walnuts and coconut. Pour over crust. Bake at 350° for 20 to 25 minutes or until set. Cool in pan and cut in squares.

You'll be sorry if you substitute the butter!

Yield: 30 bars

Edie's Brownies

5	ounces unsweetened chocolate	2½	teaspoons vanilla
1½	cups butter	5	eggs, beaten
2½	cups sugar	1	teaspoon baking powder
¼	cups flour	1	cup pecans, chopped
			powdered sugar

Melt chocolate with butter. Combine with sugar and next 5 ingredients; mix well. Pour into a greased and floured 9x12 metal baking pan. Bake at 350° for 30 minutes or until brownies slightly pull away from edges. Dust with powdered sugar and cut in small squares.

The metal baking pan is very important. Don't ask us why … Edie told us!

Yield: 30 small brownies

These brownies have been auctioned off for over $50 a pan. They freeze beautifully!

Sinful Caramel Brownies

	(14-ounce) bag caramels (about 50)	¾	cup melted butter or margarine
	(5-ounce) can evaporated milk	1	cup chopped nuts
	box German chocolate cake mix	1	cup semi-sweet chocolate chips

Preheat oven to 350°. In a double boiler, melt caramels and ⅓ cup milk. Combine cake mix with melted butter mixture and remaining ⅓ cup milk. Spread ½ of cake mixture into bottom of a greased 9x13 pan. Bake at 350° for 7 minutes. Sprinkle with nuts and chocolate chips. Spoon on melted caramels. Drop spoonfuls of the remaining cake mixture over top and pat down. Bake at 350° for 15 to 18 minutes. Cool completely before cutting into squares.

If using a pudding cake mix, bake 25 to 28 minutes.

Yield: 40 brownies

To die for!

Chocolate Amaretti Truffles

1	(8-ounce) package semi-sweet chocolate chips	1	tablespoon vanilla
½	cup Amaretto	¾	cup Amaretto cookie crumbs
2	tablespoons brewed strong coffee	½	cup cocoa
½	cup butter	½	cup instant coffee

In top of double boiler, melt chocolate chips with Amaretto and brewed coffee. Whisk in butter, 1 tablespoon at a time. Add vanilla and cookie crumbs. Set the top of the double boiler in a bowl of ice water. Continue to whisk until mixture is chilled. Place in freezer several hours. Form mixture into ¼-inch round truffles. Pulverize cocoa and instant coffee in a food processor or blender. Roll truffles in mixture. Drop into frilled candy papers. Store covered in refrigerator.

Can be frozen.

Yield: 2 dozen truffles

Flan Mexicana

8	eggs	1	tablespoon Mexican vanilla (brandy may be substituted)
⅔	cup sugar		
¼	teaspoon salt		
3⅓	cups evaporated milk	1	cup sugar

Beat eggs, add ⅔ cup sugar and salt, and mix well. Beat in evaporated milk and vanilla. In a non-stick pan, heat 1 cup sugar over medium heat until caramelized. Immediately pour into a flan or loaf pan. Pour custard mixture over. Sugar will harden and crackle as custard is added. Place pan in a shallow baking dish containing hot water. Bake at 350° for 1 hour or until knife inserted comes out clean. This can take as long as 1 hour 20 minutes. Refrigerate in pan overnight. To serve, run knife around edges of pan and invert onto platter. Top with caramel from pan. Slice thin.

For best results, prepare one day before serving. Garnish with fresh seasonal berries.

Yield: 8 to 10 servings

Banana Flan with Raspberry Sauce

Flan

3	whole eggs	1	cup milk
3	egg yolks	2	bananas, sliced
¼	cup sugar	1	tablespoon white rum
1	teaspoon lemon juice	1	tablespoon banana
½	cup heavy cream		liqueur (optional)
½	cup sweetened	1	teaspoon vanilla
	condensed milk		

Raspberry Sauce

1	(10-ounce) package	3	tablespoons sugar
	frozen raspberries,	2	tablespoons dry white
	thawed		wine or water

Beat eggs, yolks, and sugar. Add lemon juice, cream, and condensed milk. Purée milk with bananas. Add to egg/sugar mixture. Stir in rum, liqueur, and vanilla. Pour into 4 greased ramekins or 1 large flan pan; fill halfway. Place in another pan filled with water that reaches halfway up sides. Bake at 350° for 30 minutes or until blade inserted in custard comes out clean. Let stand 5 minutes. Invert ramekins onto dessert plates and unmold. Serve warm or cold with raspberry sauce. To prepare Raspberry Sauce: purée raspberries with juice, strain through a sieve, and discard seeds. Combine pulp with sugar and wine. Spoon over flan.

Use fresh raspberries and mint for garnish.

Yield: 4 servings

Butterscotch Brownies

½	cup butter or margarine	1	cup self-rising flour
	cup brown sugar, firmly	⅛	teaspoon salt
	packed	1	teaspoon vanilla
	eggs, beaten	½	cup chopped pecans

In a large saucepan, melt butter. Remove from heat and add remaining ingredients. Do not over beat. Pour in a greased 8-inch square pan. Bake at 350° for 25 minutes. Cut into squares while warm and cool in pan.

Yield: 16 brownies

Mexican Bread Pudding with Tequila Sauce

Bread Pudding

4½	cups low fat milk
½	cup margarine
3	cups apple juice
6	egg whites
2	tablespoons sugar
1	tablespoon vanilla
1	tablespoon cinnamon

1½	teaspoons ground nutmeg
¾	cup raisins, plumped in hot water

juice and zest of ½ lemon

16	cups French bread cubes

Meringue

4	egg whites
1	teaspoon vanilla
⅛	teaspoon cream of tartar

1	cup sifted powdered sugar

Tequila Sauce

½	cup margarine
1	cup powdered sugar

1	egg
½	cup tequila

To prepare pudding: in a saucepan, scald milk. Add margarine and stir until melted. Add apple juice and next 7 ingredients. Place bread in a large bowl. Pour milk mixture over bread. Mix gently. Place in a 3-quart glass baking dish. Bake at 350° for 30 to 45 minutes or until knife inserted comes out clean. To prepare Meringue: beat egg whites until foamy. Add vanilla and cream of tartar. Continue beating slowly adding sugar until stiff peaks form. Spread over bread pudding and bake at 450° until browned. To prepare Tequila Sauce: melt margarine in top of double boiler. Beat sugar and egg until light colored. Add to margarine and continue to cook for 5 minutes, stirring constantly. Do not let water boil. Remove from heat. Cool to room temperature. Add tequila and stir well. Serve over hot bread pudding.

Yield: 12 to 16 servings

¡VIVA! Tradiciones

Peppermint Ice Cream

4	eggs
2¼	cups sugar
5	cups 2% milk
4	cups half & half

4½	teaspoons vanilla
½	teaspoon salt
1½	cups crushed peppermint candy

Beat eggs. Gradually add sugar and continue to beat until mixture is stiff. Add milk and next 3 ingredients. Mix thoroughly. Pour into 1 gallon ice cream freezer. Freeze for about 15 minutes until ice cream is a mushy consistency. Stir in peppermint candy. Continue freezing according to manufacturer's instructions, or to desired consistency.

Yields: 12 to 16 servings

South Texas summers are hot! What a great reason to go for a sail, jump in the pool, and cool off with a refreshing bowl of peppermint ice cream.

Sparkling Orange Sorbet

1½	cups boiling water
¼	cup sugar
¼	cup unsweetened orange juice

¾	cup sparkling white Zinfandel or Champagne

Dissolve sugar in boiling water; cool. Add orange juice and wine. Pour into freezer can and freeze according to manufacturer's instructions. Serve immediately.

Garnish with thin orange slices or mint sprigs.

Yield: 6 servings

Hot Fudge Sauce

1	(14-ounce) can sweetened condensed milk
	cup water

⅛	teaspoon salt
½	cup sugar
1	(8-ounce) package semi-sweet chocolate chips

Combine all ingredients in top of a double boiler. Cook over boiling water until thick, stirring frequently, approximately 15 minutes.

Keeps indefinitely in refrigerator. Reheat in top of double boiler.

Yield: 2 cups

Strawberry Banana Topping

2	tablespoons margarine	¼	cup light rum
2	tablespoons brown sugar	3	bananas, sliced
2	tablespoons lemon juice	6	fresh strawberries, halved

Melt margarine in a skillet. Add brown sugar, lemon juice, and rum. Cook until sugar dissolves, stirring constantly. Add bananas and strawberries; cook until bananas are soft but not mushy, about 2 minutes.

Serve as a topping on pound cake or with vanilla ice cream.

Yield: 4 servings

Raspberry Sauce

| 2 | pounds raspberries, fresh or frozen | 3 | tablespoons sugar |
| 1 | tablespoon cornstarch | 2 | tablespoons orange juice |

Purée raspberries in a food processor. Strain through a fine sieve to remove seeds. In a small bowl, combine cornstarch with 3 tablespoons purée; set aside. Pour remaining purée into medium saucepan with sugar and orange juice. Cook over low heat until sugar is dissolved, stirring constantly. Stir in cornstarch mixture and bring to simmer. Cook 1 to 2 minutes until sauce is smooth and thick. Serve warm or at room temperature. Refrigerate unused portion.

Yield: 2 cups

Lemon Sauce

1	cup brown sugar	1	teaspoon cinnamon
½	cup butter	1	teaspoon nutmeg
1	cup water		zest and juice of 1 lemon
1	egg, beaten		

Combine all ingredients in top of double boiler. Heat thoroughly but do not boil. Simmer until sauce is thick and reduced to about 2 cups.

Serve over cake or gingerbread.

Kid's Place

Kid's

For South Texas' kids, the world is a playground — its sandbox beaches, Gulf Coast fishing holes, wildlife ranches, and learning experiences are disguised as fun. It takes just a little imagination to stack and pat pails of salty-wet sand into castles that reach tall to the sunny skies or have a thick enough wall to protect a princess inside. And that is just the beginning of all of the fun to be had at the beach. It's okay to splash and swim, look for seashells, camp out next to a roaring fire and feed the seagulls. In fact, the gulls will eat from your hand almost anywhere, whether you are pedaling down the bayfront on a bicycle or sailing in a replica of Christopher Columbus' vessel, the Niña on the Gulf of Mexico. The gulls might even follow you to Kids Place at Cole Park. That is where you can run over drawbridges, crawl through tires, swing on the monkey bars, glide down the slide, or fly on a swing. There is a wide open space where kites can soar in the sea breezes and Kids Place is right next to a pier. This is where you can put some bait on a hook and look down into the water, hoping that one of the fish swimming by will bite and you can reel it in. There are plenty more fish, birds and other animals to see here or on an expedition to the Texas State Aquarium. Sneaky alligators, long-legged whooping cranes, deer with big antlers, and mean-faced javalinas live in the water or stickly brush in the outlying areas. Some kids even raise rabbits, goats, steer, swine, turkey, capon, and lamb of their own for livestock shows. For some it is a family tradition, like so many celebrated by families of differing heritage who call South Texas home.

¡VIVA! Tradiciones

Nutty Naners

3   bananas, peeled and cut
     in half
½   cup chocolate chips
3   tablespoons milk, warm

¼   teaspoon vanilla
6   Popsicle sticks
1   cup granola

Insert stick into each banana half and freeze for 1 hour. Stir chocolate and vanilla in warm milk until smooth. If chocolate does not completely melt, microwave on high for 30 seconds. Dip frozen bananas in chocolate until evenly coated. Roll in granola. Place on plastic wrap and freeze or serve immediately.

Yield: 6 servings

For yogurt covered bananas: dip in strawberry yogurt and then roll in granola. Wrap in plastic wrap and freeze.

Gingerbread People

¼   cup shortening
½   cup brown sugar
½   cup molasses
3½   cups flour
1   teaspoon baking soda
¼   teaspoon ground cloves

½   teaspoon cinnamon
1   teaspoon ginger
½   teaspoon salt
¼   cup water
     tubes of colored icing
     cookie decorations

Cream shortening and sugar. Add molasses. In separate bowl, sift together dry ingredients. Add to shortening mixture, alternating with water. Divide dough in half and refrigerate 1 batch. Roll other out on a lightly floured surface and cut into desired shapes. Reserve leftover dough. Roll out second batch and repeat. Collect all leftover dough and roll out one more time. Bake cookies at 350° 8 to 12 minutes, until edges begin to brown. Cool and lay on waxed paper. Decorate with icing and other decorations. Store between layers of waxed paper in airtight container.

Yield: 36 gingerbread people

Fruit Roll-ups

2   cups strawberries or peaches

1   tablespoon lemon juice

¼   teaspoon cinnamon

Purée fruit until smooth. Add lemon juice and cinnamon and mix thoroughly. Spread mixture evenly on cookie sheet coated with vegetable cooking spray. Bake at 200° with the door ajar for 2 to 3 hours. Cut into strips and cover with plastic wrap.

Yield: 20 strips

Puppy Chow

½   cup butter

1½   cups creamy peanut butter

1   (12-ounce) bag chocolate chips

1   (16-ounce) box Crispix or Chex cereal

1   (16-ounce) box powdered sugar

Don't serve this to your canine friends. Chocolate is harmful to dogs.

Combine first 3 ingredients in a bowl. Microwave in 30-second segments, stirring each time, until smooth. Fold in cereal. Place sugar in paper bag. Add cereal in globs and shake until completely coated, separating pieces if stuck together. Spread on a cookie sheet to cool. Store in a sealed plastic bags.

Serve in new dog food bowls on top of ice cream. Your kids will love it!

Yield: several doggie bowls full

Peanut Crunchies

½	cup light corn syrup	1	cup crunchy peanut
½	cup sugar		butter
		3	cups corn flakes

Combine syrup and sugar in saucepan. Cook over medium heat until sugar is dissolved. Stir in peanut butter and remove from heat. Add corn flakes and mix well. Drop by rounded teaspoon onto waxed paper. Cool.

Popcorn can be substituted for corn flakes. Try pressing into greased baking dish and cut into squares when cool.

My Own Cinnamon Rolls

1	loaf frozen bread dough, thawed	½	cup brown sugar
3	tablespoons butter, melted	½	cup raisins, optional
2	teaspoons cinnamon	½	cup chopped nuts, optional

Roll out bread dough into rectangle. Brush with butter. Sprinkle with cinnamon and sugar. Top with raisins and nuts, if desired. Roll up from longest side. Slice in 1-inch pieces. Place on a greased baking sheet and cover. Place in a warm dry place to rise for 30 to 45 minutes, until doubled in size. Bake at 375° for 25 minutes.

Yield: 12 to 16 rolls

Holiday Pizza Cookie

1	package sugar cookie dough	1	can white frosting
1	cup peanut butter	1	cup M&M's

Press cookie dough onto a pizza pan. Bake according to package directions. Cool. Spread with peanut butter. Decorate with frosting and candy. Cut into pizza slices and serve.

A huge success guaranteed at your next school party!

Yield: 24 servings

Use red and green M&M's for Christmas. Candy corns and raisins for Halloween. Red hot and marshmallows for Valentine's Day.

Piñatas

2 cups flour	colored tissue paper, cut in
1 large balloon	strips
cooking spray	string
newspaper	

Beautiful piñatas can be found at many South Texas birthday parties and celebrations. They are filled with candy and hung from a tree or post. Each guest is blindfolded, handed large sticks or bats, and given a turn to try and break them open.

In a plastic bowl, mix flour with water until it is the consistency of pancake batter. Blow up balloon and tie a string around end. Tie balloon securely to a heavy object or back of chair. Spray balloon with cooking spray. Dip newspaper strips in flour paste and place them over balloon, covering it completely. Place 3 pieces of string near the base of the balloon, with edges hanging down. Apply 2 more layers of newspaper, anchoring string to piñata. Allow to dry overnight. Pop balloon and remove it from piñata. Cut edges of tissue paper to ruffle edges. Glue strips of colored tissue paper over piñata or paint with acrylic paint. Be sure to leave hole in base open and string free. Decorate piñata as your favorite animal. Create ears and hair out of colored paper. When glue is dry fill with candy and cover opening securely with tape. Tie string together and use to hang piñata.

Yield: 1 piñata

¡VIVA! Tradiciones

Kookie Burgers

1	can white frosting
2	cups sweet coconut
	red, green, and yellow food coloring

24	thin mint cookies
48	vanilla wafer cookies
1	egg white, beaten
	sesame seeds

Divide frosting evenly between 2 bowls. Color 1 bowl with red coloring and the other with yellow. Toss coconut with a few drops green food coloring. Spread one vanilla wafer with red frosting. Spread yellow frosting on separate vanilla wafer. Sprinkle green coconut on yellow frosting. Place thin mint cookies over coconut and top with red frosted cookie. Brush top of wafer with egg white and sprinkle with sesame seeds. Wrap individually in plastic wrap.

Grand for school parties.

Yield: 24 burgers

Zebra Pie

2	cups Oreo cookie crumbs
2	large bananas, sliced

1	large container whipped topping
	cherries, for garnish

Spread 1 cup cookie crumbs in bottom of glass pie pan or casserole. Layer 1 banana over crumbs and top with ½ of the whipped topping. Repeat layers, ending with whipped topping. Refrigerate several hours or overnight. Garnish with drained cherries if desired.

A wild holiday pie for los niños.

Yield: 8 to 10 servings

Play Dough

1	cup flour	2	teaspoons cream of tartar
1/2	cup salt	1	tablespoon oil
1	cup water		food coloring

Combine first 5 ingredients in a saucepan. Cook over medium heat, stirring constantly, until it pulls away from sides of pan. Divide into 4 portions and color with food coloring. Store in airtight containers.

Yield: 2 cups

Reindeer Food

| glitter | small paper or plastic bags |
| cornflakes | red and green yarn |

Ho! Ho! Ho!

In mixing bowl, combine first 2 ingredients. Carefully fill bags and tie with yarn.

Otra Vez

Texas State Aquarium

The South Texas Coast is a rich wildlife area, sprawling with many fish, sea birds, alligators and much more. To take it all in during a single cruise of the Gulf of Mexico or walk along the seashore is impossible. There is a place where you can get a glimpse of it all, The Texas State Aquarium. Representing many animal habitats of the region, from coral reefs to estuaries, it brings together a very strong display of its inhabitants in one place. Located on the southern tip of Corpus Christi Beach, the facility offers much to see and enjoy. Some sea creatures are so close you can almost reach out and touch them. Entering the aquarium requires walking through a wall of water, an experience designed to get the visitors in the mood for what is to come — an estuary, where river flow meets the salty ocean water, sandy beaches and water depths from shoreline to deep sea. In addition to the explanations of how each of the habitats supports it wildlife animals abound. Birds fly about, seashore grasses grow and an alligator might be seen poking his head out of the water, watching whoever is watching him. Anemones and starfish float in warm water, clownfish, clams and oysters in cold water and one glimpse at the sawfish shows just how he got his name. Crabs and mollusks and other shallow-water creatures live in a star-shaped petting pool. Slippery rays and sandpaper-skinned sharks zigzag around an observation area within the reach of curious hands. Animals that live near the shore, including more flounders, crabs and rays, jellyfish, and octopi live in another display area. Inside the aquarium's largest tank, islands of steel are sharks, groupers, and smaller fish swimming in schools that normally stay close to the oil and gas platforms built in the Gulf. There is even a re-creation of twin coral reefs called "The Flower Gardens". Sea turtles and river otters make their homes outside, where there is yet another stop to make — a marsh exhibit that serves as a stopover for injured animals, where they are nursed back to health. Truly a place for kids of all ages.

¡VIVA! Tradiciones

Strawberry Champagne Jelly

2 (11-ounce) cans
   strawberry nectar
4 cups sugar

1½ cups Champagne
2   (3-ounce) packages liquid
    pectin

Combine nectar and sugar in large saucepan. Bring to boil, stirring, until sugar dissolves. Remove from heat and cool 5 minutes. Stir in champagne and pectin. Strain, pour immediately into sterilized jars, and seal. Store in a cool dark place.

Three cups of fresh strawberries can be substituted for nectar. Boil fruit until soft.

Yield: 7 cups

White Zinfandel Jelly

4 cups sugar
2 cups white Zinfandel
⅓ cup orange juice

1 (1¾-ounce) package
   powdered fruit pectin

Combine sugar, wine, and juice in a large saucepan. Bring to a boil, and cook until sugar melts. Stir in pectin. Bring mixture to a boil. Remove from heat and strain. Pour immediately into sterilized jars and seal. Store in cool dark place.

Yield: 5 cups

Dancing Hot Jalapeño Jelly

2 (10-ounce) cans pickled
   jalapeños, drained,
   seeded, and chopped
1 cup orange juice

4 cups sugar
1 (1¾-ounce) package
   powdered fruit pectin
¼ cup cider vinegar

Combine peppers, juice, and sugar in a large saucepan. Boil 1 minute. Remove from heat and stir in pectin and vinegar. Stir until well mixed. Pour into sterilized jars and seal. Process in a hot water bath. Store in a cool dry place.

Yield: 5 cups

Apricot Hot Pepper Jelly

2	pounds dried apricots	1	(1¾-ounce) package powdered fruit pectin
4	cups sugar		
2	cups apple cider vinegar	1	cup diced jalapeños, seeded

Place apricots in a large saucepan with water to cover. Boil until tender, about 5 to 10 minutes. Process apricots and water in food processor until smooth. Return mixture to saucepan and add sugar. Heat slowly till sugar dissolves; boil 1 minute. Add vinegar and pectin and return to boil. Boil 1 minute. Add peppers and return to a boil. Remove from heat, immediately pour into jelly jars and seal. Process in a water bath for 5 minutes.

Try this poured over cream cheese. Also a wonderful meat marinade.

Yield: 8 cups

Jelly that will be kept on a shelf or in the refrigerator more than 3 months should be processed in a water bath to kill any bacteria.

Fresh Fridge Pickles

3	cups sugar	2-3	small onions, sliced
2	cups cider vinegar	1	bell pepper, seeded and sliced
½	cup salt		
1	teaspoon celery seed	1	red bell pepper, seeded and sliced
1	teaspoon mustard seed		
3	quarts sliced cucumbers		

Bring first 5 ingredients to a boil in a large saucepan. Remove from heat and cool. Pour over vegetables and store in a container in the fridge. Will keep for several months.

Yield: 4 quarts

The city of Corpus Christi recognizes 1852 as the year of its birth, for that was when the first city council was elected and a mayor installed.

Crème de Menthe Jelly

2¾	cups sugar	2	tablespoon fresh lime
1	cup Crème de Menthe		juice
1	cup water	3	ounces liquid fruit pectin

Combine first 4 ingredients in top of double boiler. Stir over rapidly boiling water until sugar dissolves. Remove from heat and stir in fruit pectin. Skim off foam, pour into sterilized jars, and seal. Store in a cool dry place.

Yield: 4 cups

This jelly is a perfect marinade for lamb. Coat lamb with garlic, pepper, and jelly.

Peach Chutney

3	pounds light brown sugar	¼	pound garlic, chopped
3	cups white vinegar	¼	pound ginger root,
2	tablespoons salt		peeled and chopped
4	pounds half-ripe peaches, peeled and sliced	2	lemons, sliced thin with rind
1½	pounds white raisins	1	tablespoon prepared mustard
8	serrano peppers, seeded and chopped		

Bring sugar, vinegar, and salt to boil. Add remaining ingredients and cook till thick, about 2½ to 3 hours. Pack in hot sterilized jars and seal while still hot.

Chutneys are relishes that come in hundreds of flavors and varieties. They can be somewhat expensive so homemade is always a better choice.

Fiery Fruit Relish

1	pear, diced	¼	teaspoon chili powder
1	apple, peeled and diced	¼	teaspoon cayenne,
2	celery stalks, minced		(adjust to taste)
½	teaspoon powdered	2	tablespoons lemon juice
	ginger	1	tablespoon white vinegar
⅛	teaspoon turmeric	½	tablespoon brown sugar

Combine all ingredients in a large bowl. Microwave on high for 4 to 5 minutes. Stir and microwave for 3 minutes more. Stir and cool. Store covered in refrigerator.

Excellent accompaniment to steaks and grilled tuna.

Yield: 1½ cups

Cranberry Conserve

1	(12-ounce) package fresh cranberries	2	jalapeños, seeded
1	navel orange	1	red onion, quartered
1	cup sugar	1	cup trimmed cilantro, or to taste

Combine all ingredients in a food processor. Pulse until coarsely chopped. Chill and serve.

Delicious with wild game, turkey, chicken and pork.

Yield: 4 cups

Killer Cranberry Sauce

1	cup bourbon	1	(12-ounce) package fresh cranberries
¼	cup minced shallots		
1	teaspoon orange zest	1	cup sugar
		1	teaspoon pepper

Combine bourbon, shallots and zest in a saucepan. Bring to boil over medium heat. Stir in cranberries and sugar. Cook 10 minutes or until cranberries pop open. Remove from heat and stir in pepper. Serve hot with another shot of bourbon, if desired.

Yield: 2 cups

Cranberry Chutney

1	cup water	½	teaspoon salt
½	cup sugar	1	teaspoon ground ginger
¾	cup brown sugar, packed	½	teaspoon mace
¼	cup grated orange rind	½	teaspoon curry powder
¾	cup cider vinegar	1	quart fresh cranberries
1	small onion, sliced thin (optional)	½	cup raisins
2	apples, peeled and chopped	¾	cup orange juice

Combine first 4 ingredients in a saucepan. Bring to boil, reduce heat, and simmer for 30 minutes, stirring occasionally. Add next 7 ingredients and return to boil. Reduce heat and simmer 30 minutes more. Add remaining ingredients and simmer 10 minutes, stirring well. Remove from heat and place in a sealed container until ready to serve.

Savory substitution for traditional cranberry sauce.

Yield: 2 quarts

Hoppin' Cranberry Sauce

1 (16-ounce) can whole cranberry sauce
1 (10½-ounce) jar jalapeño jelly
2 tablespoons fresh chopped cilantro

Combine all ingredients in a saucepan over medium heat. Cook until jelly melts, stirring frequently. Cool and refrigerate.

Oil of Olé

1	bunch fresh basil, washed	½	bunch fresh sage, washed
1	bunch fresh oregano, washed	1	pod garlic, peeled
1	bunch fresh thyme, washed	½	cup black pepper corns
½	bunch fresh rosemary, washed	2	cups white vinegar
		1	gallon olive oil

Place any combination of fresh herbs on a cookie sheet. Dry in a 200° oven for several hours. They should be dark and crispy. Place herbs and garlic in a bowl and cover with vinegar. Refrigerate for 3 days. Drain vinegar and place herbs and garlic in sterilized bottles. Drop in peppercorns and fill with oil. Seal with a cork and refrigerate.

This makes a special gift and can be used in recipes in place of regular olive oil.

Yield: 1 gallon

Drying of the herbs and adding vinegar kill any dangerous bacteria.

Toasted Pecans

1	cup pecans	2	tablespoons sugar
2	tablespoons vinegar	1	tablespoon butter, melted

Place pecans in small bowl. Combine vinegar and sugar; pour over pecans. Stir to coat thoroughly and let stand 15 minutes stirring every 5 minutes. Place in a shallow baking dish and bake at 350° for 10 minutes. Pour butter over and stir to coat. Bake another 10 minutes.

Hot Sweet Nuts

1	cup butter	2	tablespoons nutmeg
2	cups pecan halves	2	tablespoons cloves
2	cups whole almonds	2	tablespoons cinnamon
3	cups powdered sugar		cayenne to taste (optional)

Spiced nuts make a wonderful gift. Wrap in pretty cellophane and tie with ribbons.

In a large saucepan, melt butter and add nuts. Cook 20 minutes, stirring occasionally. Drain off butter and place nuts in a paper bag with sugar and spices. Shake vigorously. Pour into a strainer, letting excess spices fall away.

Hazelnuts can be used in place of pecans or create your own combination.

Yield: 4 cups

Rated "R" Barbeque Sauce

3	tablespoons butter	¼	cup brown sugar
1	serrano pepper, minced	1	cup catsup
2	cloves garlic, minced	1	small can V-8 juice
½	onion, chopped	2	tablespoons soy sauce
	juice of 1 lemon	3	tablespoons vinegar
¼	cup Worcestershire sauce	½	cup Tabasco

Sauté pepper, onion, and garlic in butter. Add remaining ingredients and simmer 1 hour. Baste meat, while on the grill, 30 minutes before done. Serve sauce on the side.

Rating can be lowered by omitting the serrano and/or lowering the amount of Tabasco.

The secret of tried and true barbeque is "low and slow". Temperature should be held about 175° and not above 215°.

Seasoned Salt

3	pounds Kosher salt	1	teaspoon ground turmeric
4	ounces black or white pepper	1	teaspoon ground sage
1½	ounces ground ginger	1	teaspoon ground marjoram
3	ounces paprika		
3	ounces chili powder	4	ounces garlic powder

In large mixing bowl, combine all ingredients. Store in an airtight container.

Any of these ingredients can be adjusted to individual taste. Easily doubled.

Prepare gift jars for friends ... they'll love you!

Otra Vez

Bouquet Garni

¼	cup ground marjoram	1	tablespoon crumbled bay leaf
¼	cup dried thyme		
¼	cup dried parsley leaves	½	cup dried celery leaves
2	tablespoons ground savory		cheesecloth
1	tablespoon ground sage		string

Talk about a wonderful gift!

In bowl, combine herbs and mix well. Cut cheesecloth into 36 2 to 3-inch squares; double in strength. Divide herbs equally among the squares and tie with string to make small bags.

Drop into soup or stew during the last hour of cooking time. Simmering with gravy is also a marvelous addition. Always remove before serving.

Yield: 18 bouquet garni

Beef Jerky

5	pounds flank steak (or venison)	8	large cloves garlic, minced
8	heaping teaspoons lemon pepper	½	cup Worcestershire sauce
		1	cup soy sauce

Cut meat with grain in ¼-inch strips. Mix lemon pepper with remaining ingredients. Marinate meat in mixture for 2 hours at room temperature. Spread meat on racks placed on cookie sheets to catch drippings. Dry in oven at 160° for 8 hours or overnight. Leave a crack in the oven door for circulation.

Index

¡VIVA! Tradiciones

243

Index

¡VIVA! Tradiciones